KU-175-351

COLLINS

How to succeed

STUDENTS' GUIDE

HarperCollins*Publishers*

First Published 1996

© HarperCollins Publishers 1996

ISBN 0 00 472000-8

All rights reserved

10 9 8 7 6 5 4 3 2 1

A catalogue record for this book
is available from the British Library.

Typeset by Davidson Pre-Press Graphics Limited, Glasgow

Printed and bound in Great Britain by
Caledonian International Book Manufacturing Ltd, Glasgow, G64

CONTENTS

Editorial Staff

Publishing Manager
Diana Adams

Managing Editor
Sheila Ferguson

Editors
Ian Brookes
Lorna Gilmour   Andrew Holmes
Mary O'Neill   Elspeth Summers

Science Consultant
Patricia Kelly

Computing Staff
Jane Creevy

Illustrations
Derek Marriot

Acknowledgement

The editors would like to thank the
National Extension College
for giving permission to use material
from the *Learning Skills* books.

INTRODUCTION

Collins Students' Guide has been specially written for all students at universities, colleges of higher education, sixth-form colleges, and similar institutions. The book brings together, in a single volume, advice and guidance on all the main challenges which you are likely to encounter during your course. It tells you how to succeed as you study, prepare assignments, and apply for jobs.

There are numerous factors which go to make up a successful student. Some of these cannot easily be taught or explained, but this book places particular emphasis on two key areas to which all students need to pay attention. The first of these is organization. The book encourages you to approach tasks in a thoughtful and orderly way. This sort of approach not only helps you to achieve better results but can also save you a lot of time and stress. The second important factor is communication. However much enthusiasm you have for your subject, and however well you understand the material in your course, you need to be able to express your ideas to the people who are assessing your work. This guide stresses the importance of thinking about who will read your work, and it provides a great deal of practical advice on how to get your ideas across effectively.

Collins Students' Guide will help you to succeed without having to learn a lot of complicated rules or spend hours working through exercises. It has been designed for quick reference, with tips expressed in simple terms and laid out clearly on the page. The book gives many examples to show how rules work, or how to apply the advice and tips given. It also provides specimen plans, letters, and other documents. These are intended to give you an idea of the sort of thing you might produce. You don't need to follow them slavishly. Your course might well call for a special approach, or your tutor might give you fixed guidelines to follow. Nevertheless, these examples are there to help if you have no other guidance.

This guide is designed to be kept handy so that you can dip into it when you need to. You can consult the book to help you to improve your general studying skills: for example, to help you to take notes more efficiently; or to approach assignments in a more orderly and effective manner. You may often want to use it as a reference book to solve specific problems: to check how to deal with footnotes in a report; or to look up a spelling rule which you can't quite remember. You will also find the book useful at key times when you need to assess your progress and plan your next steps: the book provides helpful checklists of things to consider before sitting examinations, before giving presentations, and before going to a job interview.

Collins Students' Guide will be a valuable resource during your time as a student. Moreover, many of the subjects covered by this book, such as report writing and job interviews, are still relevant after you finish studying, so the advice in this book will still be useful in many years' time. Good luck!

PART ONE

GUIDE TO STUDYING

PLANNING

Wherever and whatever you are studying, you will need to do some planning if you are to complete your assignments successfully and on time. You only have a certain amount of time for studying, and it is up to you to manage that time so that you spend it to the best advantage. Managing time is not difficult, but it does require a bit of thought. Effective planning can enable you to achieve better results without working longer hours. This means you have time for other things in your life besides studying.

How should I plan my term's work?

As a student, you will have to complete several assignments within the course of a term. These assignments may all have to be handed in around the same time, so planning is crucial. If you have difficulty in planning your term's work, try the following approach. It consists of four stages:

- Write down the assignments and the time period in which you have to complete them.
- Break down each assignment into a list of the main tasks you have to complete. Put these tasks into the right order.
- Draw up a timetable. Put the final dates for the completion of each assignment on this. Then add each of the tasks you listed at the previous stage. Decide on dates for each individual task. Allow time for last minute emergencies, and any assignments you don't yet know about.
- Add your other commitments to the timetable. Make any necessary adjustments to avoid bottlenecks and spread the work evenly over the term. Your final time-table might look something like the one on page 4.

Once you have set out all of your assignments for the term, you can relax. You should now be able to see how you can fit everything in, and you won't feel guilty about taking breaks from work as long as you are sticking to your timetable.

LIST OF ASSIGNMENTS FOR TERM

Assignment	Tasks Involved	Week Due
Essay 1	research; plan; writing	5
Essay 2	research; plan; writing	9
Project	research; collect data; analyse data; plan report; write report	10
Presentation on project	plan; write notes; prepare visuals; rehearse	10
Reading textbook	read units 1-6	–
Problem sheet 1	solve problems	2
Problem sheet 2	solve problems	4
Problem sheet 3	solve problems	6
Problem sheet 4	solve problems	8
Problem sheet 5	solve problems	10

How should I plan an individual assignment?

- **Define the task:** Find out as much as possible about what the finished work should look like, preferably from the person who is assessing the assignment. Otherwise you risk wasting time and getting a poor mark simply because you misunderstood what was expected. Time spent on this can save a lot of time later. Make sure you know what length the assignment should be, how marks are allocated on each section, and what method of presentation is required.
- **Assemble the resources:** All too often you find that you start work only to come to a sudden halt because you haven't got an important book or piece of equipment. Before you start work on an assignment you should identify the resources you need and make sure that they will be available when you need them. Resources may include books and journals, technical

TIMETABLE FOR TERM'S WORK

Week	Mon	Tue	Wed	Thu	Fri	Weekend
1	PARTY	Research for project	Research for project	Problem sheet 1	–	Read Unit 1
2	Read Unit 2	Hand in problem sheet	Research for project	Research for project	–	Collect data for project
3	Read Unit 3	Collect data for project	DINNER AT TUTOR'S	Problem sheet 2	–	–
4	Read Unit 4	Hand in problem sheet	Read Unit 5	Research essay 1	–	GO HOME (read on train)
5	Research & Plan Essay 1	Begin Essay 1	Finish Essay 1	Hand in Essay 1	–	Analyse project data
6	Problem sheet 3	Hand in problem sheet	Read Unit 6	Plan report	–	Begin writing report
7	Write report	Write report	Write report	Problem sheet 4	–	FRIENDS' VISIT
8	Research for Essay 2	Hand in problem sheet	Research for Essay 2	Plan Essay 2	–	Write Essay 2
9	Hand in Essay 2	Plan project presentation	Write project presentation	Problem sheet 5	PARTY	Prepare presentation
10	Rehearse talk	Hand in problem sheet	Give presentation	Hand in project report	PARTY	

equipment, CD-ROMs, survey data, and so on. If there are a number of people doing the same assignment, there may be a large demand for the available resources. Find out if you need to book resources in advance and for how long you can use them. Find out if you can take resources home with you, or if you have to use them in a fixed location. If you need to use technical equipment, make sure you know how to operate it.

- **Plan your time:** Decide what work needs to be done in order to complete your assignment. Divide the overall job into manageable tasks. Then put these tasks into the order in which you need to do them. Work out how much time to allow for each task. Decide when you will carry out each of the tasks. Try to timetable each task for a suitable time in your schedule. Keep your schedule varied and give priority to the most important tasks.

- **Make a start:** We all find it difficult to get started. It is easy to spend time on unimportant tasks as an excuse for not starting on something that needs to be done. But important tasks do not go away, and our worry and guilt get worse. But if we do tackle the work we benefit from a sense of achievement and renewed energy.

How can I maintain my enthusiasm?

All your careful planning will be wasted if you are unable to keep to your work timetable. It is easy to start with the best intentions, only to find that you lose interest, find distractions, or come up against intimidating problems. However, there are ways of planning your work so that you avoid boredom and distractions.

- Leave your work at an interesting stage so that you will want to carry on with it later.
- Leave your work at a stage where you know exactly what you need to do next.

- At the end of each study session, make a brief note to remind yourself of what you should do next.
- Study in a place where there are no distractions. This may entail going to a library, or removing distractions from the place where you normally study.
- Promise yourself a reward when you have finished all the tasks you have timetabled for the day.
- Try to get ahead of your schedule. Then if you are really fed up you can afford to take some time off.
- Keep several tasks on the go at the same time. Then you should be able to face at least one of these when you sit down to work.
- Remind yourself why you are doing your course. Think about the rewards for completing it successfully.
- Remind yourself of times when you have succeeded in the past.
- Talk about your work with your friends and teachers. Exchange ideas with them.
- Break work down into a list of small manageable steps. Tick off each individual task as you complete it. This will boost your morale as you progress towards your goal of completing the assignment.

Tips for successful planning

- Set yourself targets. These give you something to aim at and allow you a regular sense of achievement when you reach them.
- Be realistic. If you set yourself targets that you are not capable of achieving, your motivation will be reduced rather than increased.
- Build flexibility into your schedule. Don't expect that you will be able to keep to your timetable without a hitch. Something is likely to crop up unexpectedly to upset your planning, so make sure that you have scope to make some late adjustments.
- Build variety into your schedule. You can concentrate for longer if you blend reading, writing, thinking, and research.

- Don't overplan. This can be an excuse for not starting important work. If your original targets turn out to be unrealistic, you can always revise your work schedule later.
- Monitor your progress. Check whether you are keeping up with your work schedule and make any necessary adjustments if you fall behind.

You can find out more about how to plan successfully by reading *How to Manage Your Study Time* by Roger Lewis (Collins Educational, 1994).

READING

What makes a good reader?

There are many different reasons for reading. You might read for pleasure — such as when you read magazines and novels — or you might read to find out more about something, to search for a particular piece of information, or to check over something that you have written in search of mistakes. The art of good reading lies in using a reading method that is suitable for your purpose. If you are reading a novel for relaxation you might want to read quite quickly without actually taking in every word, whereas if you are trying to get to grips with a complicated set of instructions you are more likely to pore over every word. When you are studying, you need to use a number of different techniques.

Reading at speed

You can use these methods to retrieve information quickly from books:

- **Skimming** is used when you want to get a general idea of what is in the text but you don't necessarily want to read it all. It allows you to search quickly through it, finding out what areas a book covers and whether it is going to be useful to you. When you skim through a book, turn over the pages quickly and run your eye over the text looking for various pointers which will tell you about the contents of the book. In particular, look for chapter openings, subheadings, introductions, and summaries.

- **Scanning** is done at an even faster speed than skimming. It is used to look really quickly down the text for a specific thing, such as looking up someone's name in a telephone directory. The best places to scan are the contents page and the index of a book. You might also scan headings and subheadings, and use your previous experience to think where you are most likely to find what you are looking for.

Reading to understand

When you need to take in what you are reading it's very important that you fully understand what you are reading before you continue to the next section or chapter. You will have to read slowly to take in all the main ideas and facts that a chapter covers. You may even have to read a chapter more than once. It is a good idea to write down any important points as you go through it or to write a short summary of each section as you complete it.

An effective method for this sort of reading is the technique called SQ3R. In this technique you go through five stages to help you gain a thorough understanding of what you are reading:

- **Survey:** This stage is similar to skimming. Look at the title, author, date of first publication and date of this edition, to check that the book is suitable for your needs and also up-to-date. Also look at the contents and chapter headings to see which parts are relevant to you, and the introduction to see the author's purpose in writing the book. Finally check the index and bibliography to get a wider view of the book's contents.

- **Question:** Before you start to read, ask yourself what you hope to gain from this book, why you are reading it, and which parts of it are of particular interest for your purpose. If you do not think the book will help you, it might be wiser to spend your time reading something else.
- **Read:** You may have to read it more than once to fully understand it. First, get an impression of what the chapter or section is about. Next, look more closely at the details of the text, asking yourself questions about it all the time. Finally decide what you think of the chapter or section you have read.
- **Recall:** At the end of every chapter (or, if the text is difficult, part of a chapter), try to recall all the main ideas in what you have read. You may want to write down notes on the points you remember.
- **Review:** Look back over the chapter or section again to see if your recall was correct. Make a note of any points that you did not recall or any which you recalled incorrectly.

What questions should I ask as I read?
When you are trying to gain an understanding of a subject, ask yourself the following questions as you go through a text:

- What point of view is the author adopting?
- What is the basic idea in each paragraph?
- Do I understand everything the author says?
- Which parts are factual?
- Which parts are the author's opinions? Can the author back them up?
- Why did the author choose the examples, diagrams, or illustrations used in the text? What do they help to make clear?
- Do I think the text is convincing?
- Can I think of different theories that would work as well?

- What consequences flow from the author's theories?
- What consequences flow from any of the different theories I have thought of?

How can I improve my reading speed?

Reading is an important tool which can open up whole areas of information and enjoyment to us. The better we can use this tool the more rewarding it will be. It is frustrating to spend hours over books which other students seem to race through. There are several things you can do to improve your reading speed:

- Keep in practice. As with anything else, practice improves performance, so reading more often and widening the range of things that you read will expand your vocabulary and improve your reading speed.
- Use an appropriate reading technique. Different styles of text require different levels of concentration. Do not spend hours reading a text in detail if you can get the information you need from it by skimming or scanning.
- Increase your vocabulary by tackling a wider range of reading material. You will often be able to work out the meaning of an unfamiliar word from the context in which it is used. If not, look it up in a dictionary and make a note of its meaning. Try to use new words as you meet them, as this helps to fix their meanings in your mind.
- Familiarize yourself with the technical terms of your subject. When you start to read academic texts, one of the problems you are likely to come across is the unfamiliarity of the language used. Textbooks often contain words that you are unlikely to meet in everyday use and some subjects have their own specialist vocabulary. Often the book will have a glossary at the back to explain these terms. If it does not, refer to a dictionary. You may be able to get a specialist dictionary devoted to all the terms used in your subject.

Although increasing your reading speed can increase the effectiveness of your studying, remember that reading quickly without fully understanding the text is pointless. What matters most is how much of the material you read you can understand and recall.

STRATEGIES FOR LEARNING

How can I study more effectively?

Every student has their own learning style. While one style may work for one person, another person will learn more effectively by using a different method. However, research does suggest that some approaches to learning may be more effective than others. You are more likely to study successfully if you adopt an *active* approach to studying:

- Try to develop an interest in the subject by finding out about its history and how it comes into everyday life.
- Think about which facts and ideas are most important and focus your attention on them.
- Link new facts and ideas to your existing knowledge and experience. Try to relate the things you read about to examples that are familiar to you.
- Discuss your subject with other students and share ideas with them.
- Select textbooks which are clearly laid out. Good introductions, summaries, and regular headings will help you to gain an understanding of the subject.
- Ask yourself questions to help you to understand new ideas.
- Try to develop your own ideas about the subject.

How can I concentrate when I study?

- Reduce distractions from other people. Work in a place where you know you will not be interrupted, away

from televisions, phones, and friends. Tell people who are likely to interrupt you that you do not wish to be disturbed between certain hours.
- Clear your own mind of distractions. Fix definite times for doing other jobs and for leisure activities. That way, you do not have to think about these when you are studying, and you can give your full attention to your work.

How can I solve problems?

All students run into problems from time to time. These times can be very frustrating, but you can develop good procedures for solving problems. If you know that you can deal with problems as they come up, they will cause you less anxiety when they do arise. Follow these four stages:

- Think about what exactly is causing the trouble. What do you need to find out before you can solve the problem? How can you obtain this information?
- Obtain the information you need. Think about all the resources which might help you, such as books, lecture notes, or other people.
- Consider alternative solutions. What are the advantages and drawbacks of each solution? If you are not happy with any of the possibilities, then try to look at the problem from several different angles until you come up with a plausible solution.
- Choose the best solution and implement it.

How can I improve my memory?

Whatever subjects you are studying, a good memory can be a great help. All students need to learn things, whether it be vocabulary, quotations, statistics, formulae, or various types of list. Some people have a natural ability to remember a lot of facts and information, while others have to work much harder to learn things. However, there are techniques you can use to make the process of memorizing information easier and more enjoyable. You probably use some of these already:

- **Mnemonics:** These involve remembering a word or phrase in which the letters each represent facts. A well-known example is *Richard Of York Gains Battle In Vain,* which represents the colours of the spectrum: red, orange, yellow, green, blue, indigo, and violet. Another familiar one is *Every Good Boy Deserves Favour,* which represents the musical notes on the lines in the treble clef: E, G, B, D, and F. You can invent your own mnemonics to help you learn any list or series. Try to invent phrases that stick easily in the mind. It may help to base these around people or subjects that you find especially interesting. The more absurd your mnemonics are, the more easily you will be able to remember them. It is sometimes helpful to jot down any mnemonics that you are going use on paper at the start of an exam. That way you don't have to worry about forgetting them during the exam.

- **Loci:** This is a very powerful memory system which is used by gamblers to memorize long sequences of playing cards, and it can be applied to any long series of items. It works like this: imagine a journey that is very familiar to you — it may be the way to your college, or a favourite walk — and then take each of the items that you want to memorize and place it at a particular point along the journey, taking time to visualize it in its place. For example, if you were trying to memorize all the presidents of the United States, you would place George Washington at the start of the route, John Adams at a point a little further on, and so on. Run through the journey in your head a few times until you can remember where each of the items belongs. This technique requires a little concentration and persistence, but it can produce outstanding results.

- **Repetition:** This is a crude but sometimes useful method. Some things defy all other memory systems. An example is the verb endings of many foreign languages. Often the best way to learn these is simply to repeat them over and over until the pattern becomes fixed in your mind. This system of learning is now regarded as old-fashioned, and is criticized because it does not encourage people to think actively about what they are learning. However, many people who learned poems and verb endings in this way can still recite them perfectly decades after leaving school.

- **Rhyme and rhythm:** Information is easier to remember if it conforms to a regular pattern of sounds. Indeed, one of the original uses of poetry was to help people remember things in the days before writing. If you are having difficulty in memorizing something, you might try to write a few lines of verse about it to help you to remember it. The stronger the rhythm and the sillier the rhymes, the more likely they are to stick in your mind.

What other help is available?

There are a wide range of commercial products aimed at making studying easier. Whether you find them useful or not will depend on the nature of your course and your own particular style of learning:

- **Study guides:** These summarize the main points of a course, provide lists of key facts, and discuss sample exam questions. Many students find these useful as a revision aid. It is a good idea to discuss with your course tutor which of the available study guides are most helpful.
- **Study tapes:** These are particularly associated with learning languages, although they are also available for other courses. You may even want to make your own study tapes. Some students learn much better from listening than from reading and find tapes a very powerful way of learning. Tapes also have the advantage that you can listen to them while doing something else, such as cooking or exercising. For this reason, students find listening to tapes is a fairly painless way of studying. The problem is that

when you study in this way, you are not giving your full attention to your work, and so you will often need to listen to a tape several times to get the benefit of it.

- **Videos:** In the same way that many students learn well from listening to tapes, many respond well to visual images. You can supplement your study by watching recordings of plays or novels that you are studying, or programmes concerned with issues on your course. This study should be done in addition to and not in place of conventional study. Television programmes may offer an incomplete or partial interpretation of the facts, so be very careful.

TAKING NOTES

Why should I take notes?
You may need to take notes for a number of reasons:

- To help you remember something.
- To keep a permanent record of something, such as a lecture you have attended or a library book you have read.
- To help you understand what you are learning.
- To help you to concentrate. If you are listening to someone talking, your mind may easily wander; making notes helps to keep you active and involved.

How should I set out my notes?
There are two different styles that you might consider using:

- **Sequential notes:** This is the method that most students use. It involves listing the key points in order. Your notes will be easier to use if you list the points under a series of headings and subheadings. You can see an example of this method on page 16.

SIKHISM

Origins of Sikhism: Teachings of Guru Nanak; relationship with Hinduism.

History of Sikhism: The ten gurus; rebellion against Moguls; unification under Ranjit Singh; British annexation of Punjab; rise of Singh Sabha; growth as a worldwide religion.

Main ideas: worship and service more important than ritual; Five Ks.

The Five Ks:

Kesh	uncut hair
Kangha	comb
Kirpan	dagger
Kara	steel bangle
Kuccha	shorts

Key terms:
Granth – sacred book
gurdwara – place of worship
Khalsa – Sikh community

Key dates:

1469	Birth of Guru Nanak
1539	Death of Guru Nanak
1577	Foundation of Amritsar
1699	Foundation of the Khalsa
1708	Death of Guru Gobind Singh
1839	Death of Ranjit Singh
1849	Britain annexes Punjab
1873	Rise of Singh Sabha
1902	Reunification of Singh Sabhas
1984	Storming of Golden Temple

- **Nuclear notes:** This system is more visual. Write the main topic in the centre of the page. Then write related ideas around it and link them up to show their relationship to the main idea. Add links around the edges to show further relationships between ideas.

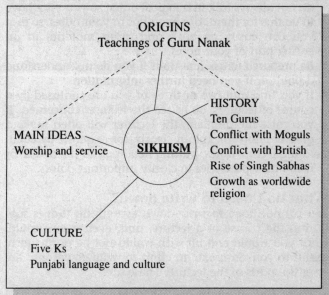

Taking notes in lectures

One of the most important uses of notes for students is to record the contents of lectures. Here are some guidelines for getting good lecture notes:

- Go to the lecture yourself. Many students are in the habit of missing the occasional lecture and copying notes from friends. A friend's notes are certainly better than no notes at all, but you are unlikely to find them as useful as notes you have taken yourself. Your friend may make notes in a style which makes complete sense to him or her, but none at all to you. Your own notes will make much more sense when you start to revise.

- Try to get a good overall picture of what is being said. Concentrate on understanding first — don't let taking notes get in the way of grasping what is being said. If in doubt, concentrate on listening rather than writing.
- Think about the logical order of the material. People do not always talk in a logical order, so you may have to do this for them. Use headings in your notes, so that you can easily go back and insert material in an earlier part of your notes.
- Be prepared to ask questions if you do not understand a point or if you need further information.
- If you find that two or three of you are confused by a course of lectures, go to see the lecturer concerned. If you raise the problem, the lecturer will often make a greater effort to explain clearly, for example by circulating lecture notes, putting headings on the board, or using transparencies to clarify important points.

What do I need to write down?

You cannot hope to write down everything that is said during the course of a lecture, and, even if you could, what you would end up with would not be particularly useful to you. So make an effort to write down only the essential parts of the lecture. These are:

- **Title:** Write down the subject, the speaker's name, and the date. This information will help you to file the notes in the correct order and to identify the notes later.
- **Main factual points:** In a science lecture these may be explanations of processes, equations, and so on. In a history lecture these may be dates and events.
- **Ideas:** These may take the form of theories about why something happens or why it is important, as opposed to the simple fact it happens. They may be widely-held ideas, or the lecturer's own original thoughts. Remember that lecturers are often also responsible for setting the exam paper, so their ideas may have some bearing on how you are expected to answer exam questions.

- **References to further reading:** Note down any references which are not included in the course bibliography.
- **Your own thoughts:** You may see that an idea relates to something you have come across in another lecture, or in your own reading, or you may find what the lecturer says particularly convincing (or unconvincing). Make a quick note of your thoughts before they go out of your head, but don't become so wrapped up in your own thoughts that you miss the next point the lecturer makes.

What do I not need to write down?

In any lecture the speaker will include a good deal of material which is intended to make the topic more easily understood, but which does not contain any new information about it. Such material may include:

- **Introductory remarks:** These often recap what was said in a previous lecture or explain the background to the subject.
- **Repetitions:** These may be intended to stress an important point.
- **Examples and analogies:** These are used by lecturers to help get information across. They are useful teaching devices, but they will not always be essential to the understanding of the subject.
- **Summaries and recaps:** These do not tell you anything new, but they do give you an opportunity to check that you have noted down the important points.
- **Digressions:** These are often introduced by words and phrases such as "incidentally" or "by the way". Digressions may be interesting but are not relevant to the matter in hand.

Taking notes from reading

You may want to take notes when you read because you only have access to a book for a short time, or because you find it helps you to concentrate on the material. You can use the following process:

- Ask yourself what you want to get out of the book, and check that the book will help you answer these questions.
- Label your notes clearly. Write down the title, the author, and the date and place of publication. If the book is from the library, also write down the classification number (given at the base of the spine) so that you can find it easily in future if you need to.
- Skim through the book (see pages 7-8) to get an overall sense of what the book is about and which parts of it are most relevant.
- Record the main topics and then note the important points under each topic. These will tend to be headings or brief statements. Where an argument, proof, or sequence of reasoning is presented, try to note down only the main steps, but don't leave out so much that you can't restate the missing processes.
- Record the major conclusions or results of each chapter.
- Record the page numbers of the sections you are noting. This allows you to double-check a point later if you need to.
- Copy out any quotations you think may be useful to you. Put quotation marks around material which you copy exactly from a book. You can then use your quotations (with an appropriate acknowledgment) in your writing without having to return to the original page to check details. This can save you a lot of time.

How can I make good use of my notes?

- Store your notes together so that you do not lose them and can find them again easily when you need them for some coursework or for revision.
- Arrange the notes in order when you file them. Keep all the notes from one series of lectures together, and arrange them in sequence. Keeping a note of the date at the start of each lecture will help you to do this.

- Read through the notes you have taken before you file them away. Do this while the subject matter is still fresh in your mind. If there is anything that you have written in your notes that you do not understand, check that it is correct and, if necessary, reword or clarify it.
- Make your notes clearer by filling out abbreviations, smartening up diagrams, and correcting any mistakes.
- Use a highlighter pen to mark key definitions, facts, or quotations that you need to learn for the exam.

Tips for success

- Be concise. If your notes are too long, you will find it tedious to wade through them either to look for a specific point or to refresh your memory.
- Emphasize important material by using underlining, different colours, and capital letters. You may not have time to use all these features in lectures, but you can add them later, before you file your notes away.
- Use abbreviations to increase your speed. Be careful that you are consistent and can remember what the abbreviations mean.
- Wherever possible put material in lists and number the points in each list.
- Use diagrams and tables wherever these allow you to represent information economically.
- Make notes in your own words. The process of converting the ideas into your own language helps you to understand the material.

You can find out more about how to improve your learning and studying skills by reading *How to Study Effectively* by Richard Freeman and John Meed (Collins Educational, 1993).

USING A LIBRARY

When do I need to use a library?

You cannot afford to buy all the books you need to read for your course. It is probably worth buying compulsory course texts, reference books, a dictionary and a thesaurus. You will need to use a library to borrow books that you only need for short periods — for instance for a particular assignment.

How do I find my way around a library?

At the start of your course you should join the library of your institution and familiarize yourself with its layout and the services it offers. You need to find out where the library keeps catalogues, reference books, bound and unbound journals, and where the stacks and shelves which hold books of interest to you are situated.

- Study the plan of the library and any leaflets that are available.
- Take advantage of any guided tours of the library that are offered.
- Ask library staff for help.
- Walk around the library yourself and get an idea of where everything is.

How are the books arranged?

Most libraries use the Dewey Decimal System for classifying books. In this system knowledge is divided into ten sections:

- 000-099 General works
- 100-199 Philosophy and Psychology
- 200-299 Religion
- 300-399 Social Sciences
- 400-499 Languages
- 500-599 Pure Sciences
- 600-699 Applied Sciences
- 700-799 the Arts

- 800-899 Literature
- 900-999 Geography, Biography, History

Each number within these sections represents a different area of knowledge. For example, 621 is Mechanical and Electrical Engineering. Further subdivisions of knowledge are indicated by numbers after the decimal point. For example, 621.43 indicates books about internal-combustion engines.

Another widely used system is the American Library of Congress system. This uses twenty-six divisions, each denoted by an initial letter. Additional letters and numbers indicate subdivisions.

How do I know if a book will be useful?

- Check whether the book is mentioned in your course bibliography. If so, has the course tutor given any indication of how useful it is?
- Look at the title, introduction, and contents page to find out whether the book relates to the subject you are studying.
- Look at the publication date to check how up-to-date the book is.
- Look at the place of publication to check that the book is likely to apply to your country.
- Check whether the author is a well-known authority on the subject.

How can I find a specific book?

- Look at the library catalogue. This is a record of the library's stock of books. You can usually access the catalogue at computer terminals throughout the library. You can search for a book by author or by title. In addition, many libraries retain their traditional card catalogues. These card catalogues may contain older material which has not yet been entered into the computerized catalogue.
- Many libraries also have access to computerized

databases on which you can search for all books on a particular subject.

- If you need a book or journal that is not stocked in the library, it can be borrowed from another library through the Inter-Library Loan network. Ask your library staff if you are unsure about how to use this system.

PREPARING FOR EXAMINATIONS

How can I cope with the stress of exams?

Most people suffer some anxiety before examinations. This is perfectly natural, and is often beneficial to your performance. For a few students, however, stress can get in the way of a good performance. If you find that stress is a problem, here are some techniques that you can use to manage your anxiety before exams:

- Remind yourself that the pressure you feel can work in your favour, enabling you to think efficiently and rapidly sift options, to plan, to recall relevant information, and so on. Many actors, musicians, and athletes say that the pressure of having to perform before an audience on an important occasion often helps them to turn in an outstanding performance. Your experience of exams can be the same. It is worth imagining your examiner as your audience — critical but ready to applaud your work.
- Remind yourself of times when you have succeeded in the past, or of things that you do well in other areas of your life. This should show you that you are competent and boost your self-confidence as you approach the task ahead.
- Visualize yourself overcoming difficulties. Identify the things that cause you to feel anxious. Take the least of these first and imagine yourself overcoming it. Then work through the other things one at a time, building up to the area of greatest anxiety.

- Train yourself to start an exam answer. For many students, the most stressful point of an exam is the sight of a blank page. You can ease this problem by practising getting started. Get a blank piece of paper and a series of exam questions. Give yourself ten minutes to come up with a plan and introductory paragraph for the first question. Do the same for each question until you become used to planning and starting answers, and the sight of a blank page loses its terror.

- Prepare early for the exam. Plan your revision well in advance, and keep to your timetable. This should save you from worrying about not being properly prepared when the exam comes around.

- Use humour to defuse your anxiety. Many students exaggerate wildly about their fear of examinations. Such exaggeration can make exams seem ridiculous, and your anxiety about them unrealistic.

- Learn to relax. There are numerous relaxation techniques that have been developed to help people overcome stress. Your doctor may be able to recommend some, or you may wish to use relaxation tapes, some of which are specifically designed to reduce exam panic.

- Use relaxation techniques during the examination if you feel a panic attack beginning. One technique is to stop work, take two or three deep breaths, and concentrate on some positive, enjoyable image.

- Talk to other students who do well in examinations. Ask them how they tackle exams and consider whether there are any things that they do which you might try yourself.

How should I approach revision?

There are as many different ways of approaching revision as there are students. You will need to try various methods before you learn which works best for you. What all revision methods should have in common is the need to plan carefully and focus on the skills that you will need for the exam. Think about these issues:

- When should I revise? Think about when you are most alert and able to study efficiently. Plan to do key revision tasks at these times. Try to get into the habit of revising at regular times. Make sure you begin your revision early and allocate yourself sufficient time to do all the necessary revision.
- How long should I revise? To remain alert and efficient during revision it is vital to take a break from work every hour or so. You may find it useful to give yourself a variety of treats during these breaks. Try to fit into your schedule one day off from revision per week. If you are up to date with your schedule, you can enjoy this free time without feeling guilty about not working; if you are behind, you can use the time to catch up.
- Where should I revise? Ideally you should revise in a quiet, well-lit place where you can leave your study materials out, and keep your revision timetable displayed on the wall.
- What should I revise? Draw up a plan based on what you need to know to pass the exam. You will not necessarily need to revise everything on the course. In fact, it will probably be a waste of your time to try to revise everything, so you need to decide how much of the course you need to revise.

How do I decide what to revise?

Find out as much as you can about the exam. Look at the course syllabus and recent exam papers. Ask your course tutor if you are still not sure about the structure of the exam. You must be sure about the following things before you plan your revision:

- What is the time allowed for the exam?
- How many questions are you required to answer in that time?
- How much time are you recommended to spend on each question?
- What form do the questions take?
- Do you have to answer the questions in a particular order?

- Can you take any aids such as a calculator, books, or a dictionary into the exam?
- Are there any compulsory questions? If so, has your course prepared you to answer these?
- Are there any topics from the course which you can safely leave out when you revise? For example, if the exam requires you to do four of eight questions, and each question is on a different topic, you can safely leave three or four topics out of your revision.
- Are the questions written in such a way that you need to know about more than one area of the course in order to answer them?

Only when you have a clear idea of the form of the exam can you judge how many topics you need to revise and in what sort of detail.

What form will my revision take?

It is not sufficient to re-read old notes and course materials. You need to work with a pen in your hand, condensing notes and continually improving your understanding of course material. Here are some active revision techniques that you might try:

- **Sorting through your notes:** You should have collected lecture notes, handouts, marked assignments, and other materials during your course. Go through all of these materials and discover which topics you have covered in detail, which topics you feel are covered only sketchily, and how the different topics in the course fit together. This exercise may reveal that you need to find out more about certain areas of the course. If you feel reluctant to pursue certain topics, find out how crucial they are. If they are not essential, you might be better to direct your energy elsewhere.
- **Refining your notes:** Rather than reading your notes over and over again, try to select and memorize the key points. Use a highlighter pen to pick out these points as you go through your notes, or make a note of key points on index cards. Concentrate on picking out key ideas,

vivid examples, key words, definitions of technical terms, useful statistics, quotations, scientific formulae, and so on. You can use different coloured highlighters for different sorts of information. It is also a good idea to make summaries of each topic in your own words.

- **Practising recall:** Try to learn information in a way which works well for you. If you have a strong visual memory, try to visualize the way that information appears on the pages of your notes. If you respond better to sounds than images, you could revise by making tapes of your refined revision notes and playing them over to yourself. Check that your revision is effective by attempting to write out important information without looking at your notes, or by rewriting material from textbooks in your own words.

- **Working with other students:** Students can benefit greatly from working together, testing each other, talking over what they believe to be the meaning of key terms, and so on. If you have a strong auditory memory this can be a particularly successful way of revising. It has the extra bonus of providing mutual encouragement and support. But beware of spending a lot of time revising with your friends if you end up talking about things other than work.

- **Putting yourself in the position of the examiner:** A key part of your revision strategy should be to review each section of your course from the standpoint of the examiner. Ask yourself what questions you would set if you wanted to test someone's understanding of this topic. If your lecturer is setting the exam questions, think about which aspects of the course he or she has laid particular emphasis on. Of course, the examiners may have a surprise or two up their sleeve, so you should not try to cut corners by hoping that certain topics come up and neglecting the rest of the course. In general, however, it is not the purpose of examiners to try to trick candidates. They are looking to find out if you have understood the important aspects of the course, and they usually want you to do well.

- **Practising exam questions:** When you feel that you
  have prepared sufficiently well, look at some sample
  questions and work out how you would tackle them in
  an exam. For most students, it is probably not a good
  use of revision time to write out full answers to individual questions (although you might want to try this
  once or twice if you are concerned about your ability
  to complete an essay in the time allowed). You can
  plan answers in note form, however, and then check
  back to see what else you might have included in
  your plan.

What if I get behind with my revision?

While you are revising, monitor your progress against
your timetable. Check that you are completing the
planned amount of revision every day. If you get behind
your schedule, take early action to catch up. There are
several things you might do:

- Reassess the amount of time you intend to spend on
  each topic. If you find that some topics are taking
  longer than you thought, think of topics that you
  could safely spend less time on.
- Put in more time on your revision until you are back
  on schedule. If you spread the extra work over several
  weeks it will only come to a short period each day.
- Use your time more effectively. Remove any distractions which stop you from revising. Make sure you are
  working towards definite goals, and that you are
  doing positive revision activities. If you are spending
  a long time on certain activities, ask yourself whether
  these activities are really necessary, or whether the
  time could be better spent doing something else.
- Delete a topic that you had intended to cover. If time
  is getting tight, you may have to revise fewer topics
  than you had originally planned. If you do decide to
  omit a topic, however, make sure that it is not an
  essential one.

TAKING EXAMINATIONS

What practical arrangements do I need to make beforehand?

- Ensure that you know the correct date and time of the exam. Check this well in advance.
- Check well in advance that you do not have two exams scheduled for the same time.
- Ensure you know the location of the exam and how you will get there.
- Check what equipment you need, and whether you have to provide it yourself. If you buy new pens, test them first to make sure they work. If you are taking a calculator into the exam, take a spare battery.
- Check that you have all the necessary paperwork, such as your exam number and receipt.
- Be sure that you know what rules operate in the exam.
- On the day of the exam, set off in good time to allow for any travel delays. Spend the time you have in hand getting ready to start, perhaps by reviewing summary notes.
- Inform the examining body of any factors, such as illness or bereavement, which may affect your performance.

What should I do when I get into the exam?

- When you get to your desk, check that you have all of the equipment you need. If anything is missing, ask the invigilator for it before the exam begins.
- Check that your chair and desk are comfortable and do not make distracting noises when you move. If you are not happy, ask for a change.
- Listen carefully to any instructions given by the invigilator.
- Do not turn over the exam paper until you are told to do so.

- Fill in the necessary personal details on the answer booklet.
- Read the instructions on the exam paper. You should already have an idea what these are from past papers, but you should check that the format is the same as you had anticipated.
- Scan all the questions before you start to write anything.
- Look closely at questions on topics you have revised in most detail. Before you start a question, check that you can do all the different tasks involved, and that you understand all the key terms in the question.
- Make a provisional decision about which questions you are going to answer. Make sure that these include all the compulsory questions, and that you are doing the appropriate number of questions in each section.
- Note down quickly any important points, possibly including a plan of how you intend to structure your answer, for each of the questions you plan to do. You can refer to these notes later when you come to start the question for real.
- Work out how much time you should spend on each question.
- Start answering the questions, keeping an eye on how much time you are taking. Do not exceed your allotted time on any question. If you find you are running out of time on one question, bring your answer to an end — taking care not to be too abrupt — and start another question.
- Allow yourself brief rests in the exam. Take the opportunity to stretch, rest your writing hand, close your eyes, and take a few deep breaths.

How do I approach essay questions?

- Do not start your answer until you are quite sure that you understand what the examiner requires. Doing precisely what the examiner requires is what distinguishes the student who answers the question successfully from the one who does not. Read the question several times, putting emphasis on different words, and see if this makes a difference to your understanding of the question.

- Be aware of the verb used in the question. You can find a list of verbs that are commonly used in essay questions, along with explanations of the sort of thing they require you to do, on pages 46-7.
- Be aware of the concepts used in the question. Underline important words in the question to remind yourself to define and analyse these when you plan your answer. The process of asking yourself questions about the meaning of key concepts often provides you with the beginning of your answer.
- Create a plan. Note all the points you need to cover and jot down any important facts.
- Make sure that the essay has an introduction and a conclusion.
- Aim to finish the essay in the time you have set yourself. You should have a good idea of how much you can write in the time available, so plan accordingly. Do not spend so much time on the early part of the question that you cannot do the second half of it justice. Keep an eye on the time and try to give equal space to all the important points.
- Lay out your work as simply as possible so that the examiner can follow your thought easily. Use short sentences, begin a new paragraph for each point, and make sure that any diagrams are clearly labelled.
- Remember that quality is more important than quantity. Provided that you cover all the important points, you should gain high marks regardless of length.

How do I approach calculations?

- Expect to use all of the information that is given to you in the question. If you get to the end and have not made use of a particular dimension, check back for a mistake in your computation.
- Watch out for information that is not stated explicitly

but must be inferred from the wording of the question.
- Take note of key words which specify the use of a particular method.
- Use the structure of the question to help you. A common style of question is one consisting of different parts which are closely connected. Each builds on the one before so that earlier work is highly relevant to the later parts.
- If the question contains the phrase "hence show..." you must use the previous piece of information in the calculation.
- Where appropriate, draw a sketch diagram. It can be a valuable aid in carrying out a calculation and prevent you from arriving at impossible answers.
- If a question specifically asks for a diagram, remember to label the diagram and give it a title.
- Give numerical answers to as many decimal places as are given the question or in standard units.
- Check that you have used units consistently and that your answer is expressed in the appropriate units.
- Put a single neat line through any incorrect working — you may still be given some credit for this if it is legible.
- Underline your final answer to indicate it clearly to the examiner.

How do I approach multiple-choice questions?

- Go through all the questions filling in any answers that are obvious to you, and which you are confident are correct.
- Go back to the questions which require more thought and work through them systematically. Do not spend a lot of time on any individual question, as each carries so few marks it is not worth puzzling over for long.
- Decide whether you should guess the answers for the questions you are still unsure about. Don't make guesses if the marking scheme penalizes you for wrong answers. If the marking scheme does not penalize

wrong answers (and most do not), you have nothing
to lose and everything to gain by guessing.

- Try to allow yourself time to check your answers and
  repeat any calculations you have made.
- Look at all the alternative answers for the questions
  you were unsure about. See if you can work out which
  errors each of the choices might be testing for.
- Keep a careful watch on your time. You must give yourself a chance to answer every question. There could be
  some easy marks waiting towards the end of the test.

What if my mind goes blank?

Many students find that one of the most frustrating
experiences in an exam is when they feel they know
something yet are unable to bring it to mind. You can
guard against this:

- If you have practised recalling facts before the exam,
  the process of recollection should work more smoothly.
- Work through any mnemonics you have devised (see
  page 13) to see if you can trigger the memory.
- Search your mind for information related to the "lost"
  item. Try to visualize the page of notes on which it
  appeared, or the voice of the lecturer talking about it.
  Think about what you were doing when you revised
  that part of the course.
- Have a quick scan through the question paper. The
  information may be contained in one of the questions,
  or be triggered by something in one of the questions.
- If you still cannot recall the point you want, don't
  spend a lot of time on it. Move on to the next answer
  or the next part of the answer, leaving a gap in the
  page. You will often find that the missing item springs
  into your mind when you least expect it. You can then
  go back and fill in the gap you have left.

What if I run out of time?

You can guard against running out of time by planning
how much time you need to spend on each part of the

exam and monitoring how much time you are spending on each question. If you do find yourself running out of time, however, stop and re-plan the rest of the exam, bearing in mind the following:

- Try to complete a basic answer for every question. It will usually be easier to gain marks for a new answer rather than squeeze more marks out of a question that has already been completed to a reasonable standard. At the very least you should provide an answer to each question in skeleton note form. Show how you would have structured your answer and what points you would have made.
- If you are spending too much time on every question, try to be more concise. It may well be that you are putting unnecessary detail into your answers.
- Try to complete any unfinished answers quickly. Do not abandon answers, but give an outline of the remaining points you wish to make and add a brief conclusion.
- If you do not have time to work out a calculation, show the method you would use even if you are not able to carry out all of the relevant steps.

What if I finish early?
Try to leave yourself five to ten minutes at the end of the exam to check your paper. Use this time to go through the following procedure:

- Check that you have answered the correct number of questions. If disaster strikes and you find you have missed out an essay, do a brief outline of the answer.
- Check that you have answered all the parts of each question.
- Go back to any gaps that you have left in your answers and do your best to fill these in.
- Quickly read through your answers and tidy up any mistakes in spelling and grammar. Add any additional points that will improve the answer.

- Rewrite any words that might be illegible to an examiner.
- Make sure all diagrams are clearly labelled.
- Check any calculations you have made.
- Check that you have filled in the correct details on the answer booklet.
- Check that you have indicated which questions you have answered and attached any loose sheets correctly.
- Continue to check your work until the end of the exam.

You can find out more about how to succeed in exams by reading *How to Succeed in Exams and Assessments* by Penny Henderson (Collins Educational, 1993).

PART TWO

GUIDE TO WRITTEN WORK

THE CONVENTIONS OF WRITING

All students need to be aware of the conventions about how to present written work. If you follow the guidelines given in this book, your work should be acceptable, although your tutor may recommend his or her own preferred style. The important thing is that you should be consistent in sticking to whichever method you adopt.

Abbreviations

There are no set rules, but observe the following guidelines:

- Use a full stop after any abbreviation that does not end with the final letter of the word.
  Co.   Esq.
- Do not use a full stop when the last letter of the abbreviation is the final letter of the word.
  Dr   Mr   Mrs   Revd
- Treat acronyms (words created from the initial letters of a phrase) as words. Do not put a full stop after each letter.
  NATO   AIDS
- Only use abbreviations in formal writing when it would look out of place to write the full form of the word.

Accents

Accents are used in many words that have come into English from other languages.

- When an accent forms part of a proper noun, it is best to retain it.
  Arvo Pärt   Bogotá
- With words that are well-established in English, the accent is usually omitted.
  precis   role
- It is helpful to retain the accent when it gives a clue to the pronunciation of the word.
  blasé   cliché

Capital letters

Use a capital letter in the following cases:

- For the first word in a sentence.
  My grant cheque has arrived.
- For the first word in each line of a poem.
  On either side the river lie
  Long fields of barley and of rye,
  That clothe the wold and meet the sky...
- To begin each word in a person's name.
  Charles Dickens
- For official, royal, and courtesy titles.
  Prime Minister   Princess Diana
- To begin all the significant words in book and film titles.
  Vanity Fair   All Quiet on the Western Front
- For trade names.
  Hoover
- For the names of countries.
  New Zealand
- For the names of peoples and languages.
  Italian   Maori
- For religions, their gods, and their holy books.
  Christianity   Jehovah   Koran
- For adjectives derived from these proper nouns.
  Islamic   Australian

Use a lower case letter rather than a capital in the following cases:

- For points of the compass.
  We were travelling north.
- For seasons.
  It was a long hot summer.
- For the first word after a semicolon.
  I like meat; my friend prefers fish.

Dates

- When writing out a date in full it is customary to use

the order *day, month, year.*
23 September 1995

- The usual practice in American English is to use the order *month, day, year.*
September 23 1995
- Using the ordinal form of the number (1st, 2nd, 3rd, etc.) is optional.
23rd September 1995
- When giving the date at the top of a letter, it is acceptable to use the shortened form of the date, with the month represented by a number, and the year shortened to two digits. There is no need to use an apostrophe before the year.
23.9.95   23/9/95
- When referring to a period of time stretching between a pair of years, it is only necessary to give as much of the second date as is needed to prevent confusion.
1996-7   1936-90   1837-1901
- The abbreviations AD and BC follow the year to which they refer. Both of these abbreviations are written without full stops.
Augustus was emperor of Rome from 31BC to 14AD.
- For approximate dates, use the abbreviation *c.* (short for the Latin word *circa*, meaning 'about').
c.1750

Italics

There are several standard uses for the italic typeface:

- To give special emphasis to a word or phrase.
e.g. This proves the murderer used his *left* hand.
- To indicate a word or phrase that is taken from a foreign language.
e.g. This is a play which captures the *Zeitgeist*.
- To indicate the Latin names of plants and animals.
e.g. Dracaena marginata is a favourite plant.
- To indicate the titles of books, newspapers, films, etc.
e.g. He played cameo roles in *Gandhi* and *Mutiny on the Bounty*.

- To show that a word or symbol is being referred to as a word or symbol.
  e.g. Listen is spelt with a silent *t*.

There are two further points to note about italics:

- If the text is already in italics, revert to non-italic (roman) text to indicate the things for which you would normally use italics.
- If you are writing by hand or typing, it is customary to use underlining instead of italics.

Numbers

- In formal writing it is customary to write out numbers in words rather than to use numerals.
- You may use numerals instead of words when the number would be excessively long to show in words (as a rule of thumb, more than two words).
  two million   2 567 683
- Use numerals for dates, addresses, and numbers in references.
  We lived at 16 Cypress Avenue until 1985.
  See chapter 7, pages 85-93.
- Use a hyphen when writing numbers from 21-99 in words, if the number consists of two words.
  twenty-one   thirty-first
- Write numbers between 1000 and 9999 without spaces or commas between the numerals. For numbers above 9999 leave a space between each set of three figures. Also leave a space between each set of three figures after a decimal point.
  4567   123 456 789   3.141 592
- Avoid confusion about the word 'billion'. This used to signify 10^{12} or 1 000 000 000 000. However, it is now customary to use the American billion of 10^9 or 1 000 000 000. Write out the amount in numerals to avoid confusion.

WRITING STYLE

It is important that you should be able to express your ideas effectively in writing. A poor writing style affects your ability to communicate with the person who is assessing your work. This can mean that you get a low mark even though your understanding of a subject is good.

Giving your work a coherent structure

A crucial part of good writing style is to impose a coherent structure on your work. This means presenting your work so that each part follows on naturally from the previous one, and all of the parts work together to express your argument. A clear structure enables the person who reads your work to follow your reasoning. There are a number of things to bear in mind:

- Plan the whole of your work before you start to write so you know where each sentence is heading.
- Deal with all the points relating to one question at the same time. Don't leave a topic and then come back to it later.
- If you are considering the points for and against a proposition, first deal with all the points for the proposition, then deal with all the arguments against.
- Group arguments and points by theme. For example, if you are considering the achievements of a historical figure, you could group these into political achievements, personal achievements, military achievements, and so on.
- Use an introduction and a conclusion to set out the structure. Set out in your introduction what you plan to do and how you plan to do it. Follow this plan in the main part of the text. Use your conclusion to review what you have done and say what this has proved.
- Sustain this structure by the way you organize your material into paragraphs. Deal with a separate point in each paragraph.

- Keep the reader in the know. At certain natural breaks in the argument it may be helpful to recap what you have done before moving on. It may also help to indicate how you intend to go about the next part of the argument.
- Use 'signposting' words to indicate the progress of your argument: words like 'firstly', 'in addition', and 'finally' show that you are progressing through a series of points; 'moreover' indicates that you are bringing in a supporting point; 'however' introduces counter-arguments; 'therefore' indicates that you are drawing a conclusion.
- Use 'signposting' sentences to show that you are moving from one section of the argument to the next. For example, if you are moving from a series of points in favour of a proposition to a series of points against it, then tell your reader so: *While there are, therefore, many arguments in support of Smith's statement, there are also several objections that can be raised...*

How do I organize material into paragraphs?

- Each paragraph should contain one clear controlling idea and sentences which provide support to this controlling idea. This controlling idea is usually expressed in what is sometimes called the 'topic sentence'.
- The topic sentence is usually — but not always — placed at the start of the paragraph. It makes clear what point the paragraph is to discuss. The topic sentence summarizes the content and subject matter of the paragraph. It helps the reader to see quickly what point is to be made in the paragraph, and prepares the reader for what follows.
- The topic sentence should be supported by the other sentences in the paragraph. Each of these should in some way add to the topic sentence. These sentences may, for example, explain ideas raised in the topic sentence, define terms more fully, or give supporting detail.
- Supporting sentences often include examples which help the reader to grasp the controlling idea of the paragraph.

- It is often effective to finish a paragraph with a sentence that sums up the paragraph or prepares for the next one. However, not all paragraphs will need this, and a concluding sentence should not simply repeat the topic sentence.

How do I construct effective sentences?

- Think carefully about exactly what idea you intend to convey, how it follows from the previous sentence, and how it prepares for the next one.
- Don't try to say too much in a single sentence. If a sentence seems clumsy, see if it works better as two shorter sentences. In general, each sentence should convey a single idea.
- Vary the length of your sentences. Short sentences are often clear and forceful, but too many of them can produce an unnatural, choppy effect.
- In longer sentences use conjunctions like 'whereas', 'because', and 'although' to indicate the relationship between the different parts of the sentence.
- Use parallel structure when dealing with a series of items in a sentence.
  The transmission is faulty, the tyres are unsafe, and the exhaust is cracked.
- Use parallel structure to highlight contrasting items in a sentence.
  A star moving towards us shows a blue shift in its spectrum, whereas a star moving away from us shows a red shift.
- Use word order to give emphasis. First and last words often carry special emphasis. The sentence *We must avoid war at all costs* can be given additional thrust if the key word is moved to the start of the sentence.
  War must be avoided at all costs.
- Avoid saying the same thing by two different means in a sentence. Make every word count.

Clear expression

- Make sure you have a thorough understanding of

your subject matter. If you don't understand what it is that you want to say, you are unlikely to be able to convey your meaning to the reader.

- Keep your reader in mind. Don't spell out things that the reader already knows, but give sufficient background information so that he or she can follow your argument.
- Identify important terms and expressions and define these at an early stage, so that the reader will understand their meaning when they occur later.
- Vary your vocabulary. Often you will have to refer to the same object many times in the same paragraph. Use pronouns and synonyms in order to avoid excessive repetition of the name of the object.
- Keep it simple. Don't try to use complicated technical language or unfamiliar foreign phrases for their own sake when you can express yourself in plain English.
- Only use words if you are confident about the correct way of using them.
- Avoid colloquial language and slang.

How can I improve my writing style?

- Sentences do not always come out right first time. They may need to be worked on. Try to phrase them in several different ways until you are happy with the result.
- Check your work by reading it aloud to yourself. Try to imagine someone else reading it for the first time, and note any sentences which seem awkward or unclear.
- Type or word-process your work. Then when you read back what you have written it is not so personal. You will be able to look at it more objectively and see things that might be improved.
- Take note of your tutors' comments on your writing style and identify your strengths and weaknesses.
- Be aware of common mistakes. Many of these are listed in the *Guide to the English Language* on pages 73-100.

- Read widely, and think about the way that other writers use words effectively.

WRITING ESSAYS

Where do I start?
When you start work on an essay, look closely at the wording of the title and ask yourself the following questions:

- What is the general subject matter of the question?
- Do any words in the question indicate how I am expected to discuss this subject?
- Are there any important ideas which need to be defined and analysed in the essay?
- Which aspects of the subject do I need to find out about before I can write the essay?

Key verbs
The verb often gives a precise indication of the way you are expected to discuss the subject matter. The following verbs appear frequently in essay questions. Make sure that you are quite clear about the meaning of each of them:

- Analyse   Break up into parts; investigate
- Compare   Look for similarities and differences
- Contrast   Bring out the differences between
- Define   Set down the meaning of a word or phrase
- Describe   Give a detailed account of
- Discuss   Investigate, giving reasons for and against
- Distinguish Indicate the differences between
- Enumerate   List in order
- Evaluate   Give a judgment based on evidence
- Examine   Look closely into
- Explain   Give reasons for
- Explore   Consider from a variety of viewpoints

- Illustrate   Make clear by using examples
- Interpret   Show the meaning of
- Justify   Reply to the most obvious objections about
- Outline   Give only the main features of a subject
- Relate   Tell in order
- Relate to   Show how one thing is connected to another
- State   Present in a clear form
- Summarize   Give a concise account, omitting details
- Trace   Show the development of a topic from some point

Collecting ideas

Once you have a clear idea of what the question requires you to do, think about what you already know about the subject and you what you need to find out. Here are two techniques that will help you to collect ideas and information for your essay:

- **Brainstorming**: Clear away all your books and papers. Find a blank sheet of paper and a pen. Look at the essay topic and write as many points as you can in five or ten minutes. Don't worry if some of what you write seems wild or irrelevant. Most students are surprised at what they can produce. Brainstorming helps you to explore the topic and to uncover ideas which you can later rework and develop.
- **Probing**: Write down a list of questions to which you require answers, and think about where you might find the answers to these questions. These questions will guide your research when you collect the material for your essay.

These techniques don't have to take a lot of time. They will help you to direct your research profitably and, in the long run, they may reduce the amount of time you spend planning and drafting your essay.

Where can I find material for the essay?

There are many different places where you can gather material for an essay. Here are a few ideas:

- Look at your course notes.
- Look at the items on the reading list.
- Look at other books on the subject in the library.
- Check to see if there are other useful books in different libraries.
- Use your own knowledge of the subject.
- Scan journal articles.
- Look at entries in encyclopedias and reference books.
- Talk to people who have expertise or experience in the subject.
- Listen to radio and television programmes on the subject.

Do I need to make a plan?

After you have spent some time gathering information, draft a plan for your essay. There are several reasons for doing this:

- If you have a plan you can start writing your essay with a clear sense of what needs to be done.
- A plan will lead you to arrange your material into paragraphs when you start writing.
- A plan will help you to break the task of writing an essay into manageable chunks.
- Following a plan ensures you deal with all the important aspects of the question and do not waste time on unimportant items.

How do I make a plan?

- Survey all the information you have collected during your research.
- Sort this information, deciding which points to develop and which to discard.
- Select the most promising material and decide how to group it into chunks.

- Decide how important each chunk is in answering the question.
- Consider how the various chunks relate to each other.
- Arrange the information into a sequence so that all the information follows in a logical order.
- Write out a plan for the essay. Your plan should include an introduction, a sequence of paragraphs, each dealing with a different point, and a conclusion.

The plan on page 50 shows one way of planning an essay concerning differences in society between 1900 and today. In the plan the points are grouped into categories and listed according to their importance.

How do I structure essay questions?

It is not usually sufficient simply to write down information. You need to use the information as evidence in an argument which leads you towards making a particular verdict. There are two main approaches to answering essay questions:

- **The 'jury' method:** In this method you put forward the evidence on both sides of the argument and end with a concluding paragraph giving your verdict. Your verdict should not be a simple opinion but a considered judgment based on the evidence you have set out.
- **The 'advocate' method:** In this method you put your verdict in your opening paragraph and build the rest of your essay to support your verdict. This approach has the advantage of signposting to the assessor what view you will be supporting and how strongly. Set out the evidence both for and against your view in the same way as in a jury essay.

If on reading through your essay it seems to be just a long list of facts, you may have missed the point. Check the title again, paying special attention to the verb, and see if you can make any changes to show how facts lead you to make your verdict.

Enumerate the changes that have taken place in British
society since 1900

Introduction

1 Material differences

   a housing

   b clothing

   c costs of goods and services

   d food

2 Changes to institutions

   a commercial: (i) banks; (ii) insurance

   b educational: (i) schools; (ii) colleges; (iii) universities

   c political

   d legal

3 Changes in employment

   a decline of old industries:
      (i) rail; (ii) heavy engineering

   b rise of new technology:
      (i) microcomputers; (ii) electronics

   c women's work – service industries

4 Other changes

   a different expectations

   b faster pace of life

   c environmental awareness

Conclusion

What should I put in the introduction?

The introduction is usually a single paragraph of 50-200 words. It should include the following:

- A clear statement of the subject you are going to discuss.
- Definitions of any terms that the reader needs to understand in order to follow your argument.
- A statement of what you think the question requires you to do and how you are going to go about answering it.

A good introduction should make the reader want to read further to see how you accomplish the task you have set for yourself.

What should I put in the main part of the essay?

- Follow the plan you have made, giving a paragraph for each point.
- Try to link the paragraphs together so there are no abrupt changes of subject.
- Follow the tips on pages 42-3 about giving your work a coherent structure.
- Keep in mind the title of the essay, and make sure that all the points you make are relevant to it.

What should I put in the conclusion?

The conclusion should be about the same length as the introduction. Consider these points:

- The conclusion should not simply repeat what has already been said.
- The conclusion should draw together all the main points made in the essay.
- The conclusion should refer closely to the question and show how the points you have made lead you to arrive at your verdict.

- Try not to sit on the fence when making your verdict. Show that you are capable of making a judgment and arguing a case persuasively.
- You can finish with some impact by introducing a new perspective to the subject in your conclusion. This can be done by relating the topic to other significant issues, or by indicating an area for further study.
- A quotation or a question can be an effective way of finishing an essay.

Quotations and references

In the course of an essay you will probably want to quote from various sources. Here are some guidelines for presenting quotations:

- Put inverted commas around quotations to show that the words are not your own.
- A brief quotation may be included inside a sentence.
  Macbeth says life is "a walking shadow".
- If you are quoting poetry, indicate line breaks by an oblique stroke.
  Macbeth calls life "a walking shadow, a poor player, / That struts and frets his hour upon the stage".
- If you are quoting a large portion of poetry, keep the lines in their original form, and introduce the quotation with a colon. Begin the quotation on a new line and indent the lines you are quoting.
  As Macbeth says:
    "Life's but a walking shadow, a poor player,
    That struts and frets his hour upon the stage,
    And then is heard no more".
- If the quotation begins in the middle of a line of poetry, indicate this by starting the quotation to the right.
- If you want to quote a large portion of prose, begin the quotation on a new line, indent both margins, and introduce the quotation with a colon.
- If you are typing and using double spacing, it is usual to change to single spacing when giving quotations.

- Indicate the source of the quotation, either by inserting a number in the text as a key to a footnote, or by giving the author's name and the page number in brackets.
- Indicate the source of any important ideas you use, even when you do not quote the author directly.
- If you are quoting from a play, include the act, scene, and line numbers.
- List the sources of all your quotations at the end of the essay, giving the author, title, and place and date of publication. This list should also include all books and other materials that you consulted during your research and which you found useful when writing your essay.

Writing essays in examinations

In examinations you have less time to research, plan, and write an essay. You need to make certain adjustments:

- You will not be expected to give a lot of detail in your answers. Stick to the most important points.
- Don't give references or footnotes, but you should still indicate the author of any quotations.
- Follow the guidelines for exam essays given on pages 31-2.

> You can find out more about writing successful essays by reading *How to Write Essays* by Roger Lewis (Collins Educational, 1993).

WRITING UP EXPERIMENTS

What is the aim in writing up an experiment?

Your write-up should be a clear, concise account of why and how an experiment was performed, what results were obtained, and what conclusions can be drawn.

When you write up an experiment you should put yourself in the place of a reader who has not done the experiment and knows nothing of its aims. The finished account should be self-contained and independent of any manual you may be following (unless you have been instructed that you may refer to one).

How should I set out a write-up?

The write-up usually follows the sequence of headings given below, although the emphasis may vary depending on the type of experiment:

- **Title:** A short sentence indicating what the experiment is about.
- **Aims:** A brief summary, in one paragraph, of the aims of the experiment.
- **Introduction:** Give details of the theory behind the experiment, including equations which will be used in the calculation of results, chemical reaction pathways, principles behind the method used, and so on. An experiment is formulated on the basis of a theory or assumption – for example, that reacting A with B will give C, or that plotting x versus y will give a linear relationship with gradient equal to z, where z is a useful quantity to measure. Explain such background information in the introduction.
- **Experimental:** A description of what physically occurred during the experiment: what you did and what happened as a result. It should be written in the passive form (e.g. *the flask was weighed* rather than *I weighed the flask*). This section may be further subdivided into categories such as: **description of apparatus**, including diagrams wherever this aids clarity; **synthesis of compounds**, which should include yields of products, given as a percentage of the theoretical yield possible, and any 'characterization' performed (i.e. analysis that confirms the product is what you intended to produce); **method** or **procedure**, saying how you went about preparing samples or taking measurements, including any special precautions or techniques that you used.

- **Results:** Where possible, results should be presented in tables and graphs, even if they are qualitative. If external factors such as room temperature and pressure could influence the result, these should be quoted.
- **Discussion:** Compare your experimental results with the theory or expected behaviour, and describe and explain any deviations from this. Calculate any required quantities, giving explanations of the calculation method and any assumptions and approximations made. Values of quantities should be included in complete sentences. Repetitive calculations should not be given in detail, but an illustrative calculation should be presented. Sources of random and systematic error, limitations of the apparatus, and suggestions for improvements should be included. (The results and discussion sections may be combined together, but you should make a clear differentiation between raw results and calculations or processing based upon them.)
- **Conclusion:** Give a simple and concise summary of the conclusions which you draw from the experiment with a clear indication of their limitations.
- **References:** This is an optional section for more advanced reports. You may refer to the work of others in the introduction, experimental, and discussion sections to explain theory, as a source of data, or for comparison of results, by putting a marker in the text in brackets or as a superscript. The marker may be a number or the author's surname plus the year of publication. If you do this, add a list of references at the end. This section contains a list of the markers with their corresponding references in full. Provide enough details for a reader to be able to find the reference in a library.

Tips for a successful write-up

- Neatness in your write-up is of great importance. You may have obtained very good results, but you will have wasted your time if you do not convey this by writing them up clearly and intelligibly.

EXPERIMENT:

Determination of the acceleration due to gravity by means of a simple pendulum.

by: S. Dent   14th February 1996

Aim. To measure the acceleration due to gravity, g, by means of its relationship to the simple harmonic motion of a simple pendulum.

Introduction. The ideal simple pendulum consists of a point mass suspended by a weightless string, represented in Figure 1.

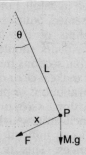

Figure 1.
The ideal simple pendulum
and forces acting upon it.

For an angular displacement, θ, the restoring force, F, acting on the point mass, M, at P along the arc, x, is given by:

$$F = -M \cdot g \cdot \sin\theta \qquad (1)$$

If θ is small, this approximates to

$$F = \frac{-M \cdot g \cdot x}{L} \qquad (2)$$

As force is equal to mass acceleration (*a*), then, from equation (2):

$$\frac{-g \cdot x}{L} = a \qquad (3)$$

Thus the acceleration of the mass, M, is proportional to its displacement from the equilibrium position and its motion is simple harmonic, for which the periodic time, T, is given by:

$$T = 2\pi \sqrt{\frac{L}{g}} \qquad (4)$$

Experimental.

<u>Apparatus</u> Retort stand, metre rule, lead bob, stopwatch.

<u>Procedure</u> The apparatus was set up as shown in Figure 2, with the cork clamped in the retort stand and the pendulum overhanging the bench. The length L was measured as the distance from where the string emerged from the cork to the centre of the bob.

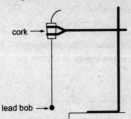

cork →

lead bob →●

Figure 2.
Apparatus set-up.

Starting with L approximately 20 cm, the time for 20 complete swings, 20.T, was measured using the stopwatch. The displacement of the pendulum was kept small. The length L was then increased by about 10 cm and the procedure was repeated. Measurements for 10 different lengths were taken.

Results and Discussion. Table 1 shows the results of time for 20 swings (20.T) for different values of pendulum length, L. T, the time for one swing, and T^2 have been calculated and are also given in the table.

Table 1. Time taken for 20 swings of the pendulum (20.T) for various lengths (L) of pendulum.

$\dfrac{L}{m}$	$\dfrac{20.T}{s} \pm 1.0$	$\dfrac{T}{s} \pm 0.050$	$\dfrac{T^2}{s^2}$
0.233	19.0	0.950	0.90 ± 0.10
0.305	22.0	1.100	1.21 ± 0.11
0.422	26.0	1.300	1.69 ± 0.13
0.503	28.5	1.425	2.03 ± 0.14
0.621	32.0	1.600	2.56 ± 0.16
0.730	34.0	1.700	2.89 ± 0.17
0.810	36.0	1.800	3.24 ± 0.18
0.908	38.0	1.900	3.61 ± 0.19
1.030	42.0	2.100	4.41 ± 0.21
1.130	43.0	2.150	4.62 ± 0.22

From equation (4), it can be seen that a plot of T^2 versus L should give a straight line with a gradient of $4\pi^2/g$, from which g can be obtained. Figure 3 shows this plot for the measured data; the response is linear within experimental error, substantiating the theory that the pendulum is undergoing simple harmonic motion. The gradient of the line, obtained by linear regression, is equal to (4.184 ± 0.068) s^2m^{-1}, giving g = (9.4 ± 0.2) ms^{-2}.

Possible sources of error in the measurement are air friction on the bob – as it is not a point mass as assumed in the calculation – and slow reaction times when using the stopwatch.

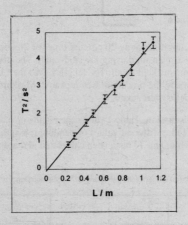

Figure 3. Plot of the square of the time of swing versus the length of the pendulum.

Conclusion. The accleration due to gravity has been determined using a simple pendulum and found by this method to be (9.4 ± 0.2) ms^{-2}.

- Write clearly in ink, or type. Some computer word processing packages are very useful for scientific applications, allowing equations to be put in easily and graphs to be imported from other programs.
- Subdivide sections where this aids clarity. Make all divisions obvious by using a combination of leaving a blank line, inserting an underlined heading, or using a numbering system for the different parts.
- Label and number all figures (diagrams and graphs) and tables fully and clearly. Refer to them in the text by number (e.g. *Figure 2 shows...*).
- Make all diagrams large and clear so the reader can make out all details.
- Number mathematical and (bio)chemical equations so that they can be referred to by that number later in the text.
- Adjust the axes on graphs so that the data points fill the graph. Axes do not need to include zero unless an intercept is required.
- Always include units with all quantities, whether in the text, table column headings, graph axes, or diagrams. Use a combination of multiples of SI based units (e.g. m, mm, s, kg, mol, kJ) unless other units are explicitly requested. In this way, you are less likely to make mistakes in your calculations.
- Indicate the errors associated with measurements and results. Give possible sources and an estimate of their magnitude. Consult a textbook to see how errors may be propagated.
- Be sensible in the amount of significant figures you quote with final results. Errors should only be quoted to one (or maybe two) significant figures and the result should be quoted to the same precision as the error: for example, $T = (25.9 \pm 0.3)$ °C. However, it is best not to round up figures during the calculation as this can introduce systematic errors.
- For a professional touch, add references and compare your results with those cited in text books and scientific journals.

WRITING REPORTS

As a student you may have to write two sorts of report. These are:

- A short document presenting the results of an investigation.
- A formal dissertation or thesis submitted as part of your course.

Learning how to write reports is a useful skill because you may well find later that you need to write reports as part of your job.

Collecting information

You may have to spend a lot of time collecting information from various sources before you even think about writing your report. You may end up with a large amount of data, so you need a method of recording all the information before you can arrange it into your final report. Use one of the following methods:

- For a short project, write each separate piece of information on a sheet of A4. Leave a space between each item. Add details about the source of your information. Write on one side only.
- If you have access to a word processor, open a file and enter the information on that as you would if you were writing on paper.
- Collect the information on file cards and a store them in a box. You can buy these cards and boxes from stationery shops. Write each piece of information on a separate card together with the source. Write on one side only.
- An economical variant of this method is to make your own cards from A4 paper. Fold a sheet of A4 paper in half and tear it. Then repeat the process to produce four sheets of paper each about the size of a file card.

You can store these in a shoe box or hold them together with bulldog clips and elastic bands.
- If you have access to a database package on a word processor, input the data onto that.

Organizing the information

- If you have collected information on A4 sheets, cut the sheets into slips so that each piece of information appears on a separate slip of paper. Move these around until you have them in the order you want. It may help if you stick them on larger sheets. You will have to add pieces to fill in gaps and to provide links between the different pieces of information, and you may find you do not use all of the information you have gathered.
- If you have stored information on a word processor, use the 'cut and paste' facility to move the text around on the screen until the various pieces of information are in the order you want. You now have the outline of your report, and you can change and add to the text until you have it in the form you want to submit.
- Arrange the file cards (or pieces of paper) so that they follow in a coherent order. If each card deals with a different point, use the cards to act as a guide to paragraphing when you start writing the report.
- Use the 'merge' facility in your database package to move the information into a word-processing file. Use this file as the starting point for writing your report.

What method should I use for arranging the information?

The task of arranging the information may seem intimidating at first, especially if you have collected a lot of data. If the order for the information is not immediately clear, follow this process (it is assumed you are using cards, but the process can be adapted to whichever method of collecting information you have used):

- Look through the cards to see what sort of information you have collected. Does this cover the terms of reference of the report? (If not you may have to collect more information before you go any further.)
- Decide on wide categories into which you can sort the cards – these will probably be the separate sections of your final report. For example, if you are writing a report on the applications of a scientific process, the categories might be 'industrial applications', 'domestic applications', 'military applications', and so on.
- Sort the cards into these wide categories. If you have any that do not fit they might be included in a 'miscellaneous' category, or be made a category by themselves, or you might decide that this information is not really important for your report. If any cards seem to fit in two categories, you may need to make a cross-reference. Make a card to indicate this and put it in the appropriate place.
- Take all the cards dealing with one category. There should now be a manageable number. If not, divide further into subcategories. These subcategories may appear as subsections in your final report.
- You are now in a position to arrange the cards into the order in which you want the information to appear.

How should I set out a report?

The layout of your report will depend on its length and readership. If it is a short report in a relatively informal situation you may not need to follow the standard formal layout. For a long, formal report, you will need to consider most of the items listed below. If the report is a dissertation submitted as part of your course, you will probably be given guidelines about layout and presentation. Be sure to read these carefully and follow them. The standard layout is as follows:

- **Title page:** This contains the title of the report, the name of the author(s), and the date of the report.

- **Abstract:** This is a brief summary (not more than one page) of the whole report, stating the aims, methods, and conclusions.
- **Contents:** List the different sections of your report, and give the page numbers where they can be found. (An example of this is given on page 64.)
- **Introduction:** Tell the reader what the subject and purpose of the report is, and explain the method you will use.
- **Main text:** This contains the information you have collected for the report. It is usually helpful to set out the text in a number of sections, with each section dealing with a separate issue.
- **Conclusion and recommendations:** This is a brief, easy-to-understand section saying what you have found and what you think needs to be done. The recommendations may sometimes be listed in a separate section.
- **Appendixes:** These contain additional information that has been omitted from the main text, but which may be of interest to some readers.
- **Notes:** These give details which would be too cumbersome to include in the main text.
- **Bibliography:** Give a list of books, journals, news-papers, etc. that you have found useful during your investigation or that you have referred to in the text. For each item include details of the author (with initials), title, and the date and place of publication. The items should be listed in alphabetical order of authors.

Labelling sections

- Label each of the different sections in the main part of the report. This helps you to organize your material and the reader to find his or her way through the report. It also allows you to refer easily to other sections of the report.

Evaluation of a Word Processing Package

- You can use numbers or letters to label the different sections.
- A popular method is the 'decimal' system. Use a number for each main section. If you have subsections inside main sections, add a second number after the section number. For example, if section 3 is split into four subsections, number these 3.1, 3.2, 3.3, and 3.4. (This is the method that is followed in the example on page 64.)
- Don't overuse subdivision of sections. Too much numbering only confuses the reader. It is unlikely that you will need to use more than two levels of subdivision. A short report may be effective without any system of numbering at all.
- Stick to the same system throughout the report.

What should I put in the conclusion?

- Remind the reader what the purpose of the report was. This will have been set out in the introduction.
- State the main points arising from the report.
- Make conclusive judgments about the issues you have been investigating.
- List any recommendations about action that you think needs to be taken and who should take it.

What sort of material should be included in appendixes?

Include as appendixes anything that is relevant to the report but which would interrupt the flow of the argument if it appeared in the main body of the text. For example:

- Glossaries giving the meanings of technical terms used in the report.
- Detailed breakdowns and analysis of results.
- Statistical data.
- Specimen forms and documents.

If you have more than one appendix in the report, label each one with a number or letter.

When do I need to give footnotes?

If you can avoid using footnotes, do so. They can be confusing to the reader. However, sometimes you will want to use them to include information that does not fit neatly into the text. Footnotes can be used:

- To give the source of your information. If you are referring to a written source, give full bibliographical details in the note, unless the source is listed in your bibliography, in which case give the author and date only. Give the page number(s) of the relevant part of the source.
- To give a fuller explanation of a point.
- To qualify a point by giving arguments against it.

Where do I place footnotes?

Insert numbers in the text at the places to which the notes refer. Then put the numbered footnotes in one of the following places:

- At the foot of the page if you have this facility on your word processing package.
- At the end of the section.
- All together at the end of the report, before the bibliography (if you have one).

How do I deal with illustrations, graphs, and tables?

Illustrations can condense a large amount of material into a small space. They can, therefore, be very useful both to you and to your reader. You may consider using pie charts, bar charts, graphs, tables, plans, maps, photographs, and labelled diagrams in your report. When dealing with illustrations, think about the following points:

- Use illustrations only if they make the point more effectively than the written word.
- Position the illustration carefully in the text, so that it is not separated from the discussion it refers to.
- Consider whether the illustration would work better as an appendix.
- Introduce the illustration in the text and explain its significance.
- Draw diagrams using a suitable scale so that the information in them can be easily understood. Give details of the scale used.
- Keep illustrations simple. Don't try to convey too much information in one diagram.
- Use labelling to make diagrams easy to understand.
- Provide captions to tell the reader what each illustration shows.
- If you have more than one illustration, number them "Figure 1", "Figure 2", etc. You can then use these numbers in the text to make it clear which illustration you are referring to.

How should the report be presented?

Once you have written the text, you still need to make sure the report is suitably presented. Think about these things:

- **Typing:** Does the report need to be typed? Can you do this yourself, or will you have to get someone else to do it? If so, what instructions do you need to give the typist?
- **Layout of pages:** Give a generous margin on all sides. (You may need to add extra space at the margin if the report is going to be bound.) Use double spacing, except for long quotations and tables. Think about the most effective way to use bold type and underlining to show section headings, and make sure you are consistent in the way you have arranged your work.
- **Checking:** Check that there are no mistakes in spelling, especially if you have got someone else to type your report. Also check that illustrations appear

correctly, and that footnotes, section headings, and appendixes are numbered in the correct order.

- **Cover:** You might enclose the report in a folder or a plastic wallet. A formal dissertation may have to be bound. If so, you should be given instructions on where to get this done.

Tips for success

- Insert 'signposts' at the beginning of each section of the report. Especially in a long report, the reader needs to be reminded of what has gone before, and told what the new section is concerned with.
- Remember that it is your job to help the reader. If a feature such as an appendix or footnote will make it easier for a reader to use your report, then include it.

You can find out more about writing successful reports by reading *How to Write Reports* by John Inglis and Roger Lewis (Collins Educational, 1994).

GIVING A PRESENTATION

It may seem strange to find a section about giving a verbal presentation included in a chapter about writing. However, to be able to speak effectively you need to be able to organize your material into a coherent and easy-to-follow structure in much the same way as when you plan written work.

How should I prepare to give a presentation?

You need to plan spoken presentations thoroughly. Consider the following points:

- **Topic:** Think about the subject of the talk. Are you comfortable talking about it? Is the topic relevant to the audience?

- **Audience:** How large is your audience going to be? What is their background? What are their interests? What will they want to know about your topic? What might they already know about it?
- **Language:** Will you be using difficult or technical language that might confuse your audience? Do you need to use clear, precise language to inform your audience about facts, or lively, persuasive language to convince them of your argument? Are you going to use any emotive or extreme language which could alienate your audience or turn them against you?
- **Time:** When exactly is the talk to take place? How much material will you need? Will there be time for a question-and-answer session after the talk itself?
- **Venue:** Where is the talk to take place? Is the venue suitable for the audience, and, if not, can you arrange to change it?

Organizing the venue

Try to take a look at the venue before giving your presentation. Ask yourself these questions:

- Are there enough seats? Can you bring in extra seats from elsewhere?
- Where will you be speaking from? Will you (and any visual aids) be visible to everyone?
- Will everyone be able to hear you? Will you need a microphone? Will you have to speak over a lot of background noise?
- Is the room suitable for audiovisual aids?
- Can you see a clock so that you can pace your talk?

How can I make sure the audience follows the presentation?

It is very important to have a clear structure. It will make your talk easier to follow and more memorable. In general, a talk should have an introduction in which you state your point or points, development of these points, and concluding remarks which tie it together and make the final point clear.

- Start by outlining what your talk is about and how you are going to present it.
- Deliver your talk in the way you indicated in your introduction.
- Use linking sentences so one point leads to another. Otherwise they may seem unconnected, and your talk disjointed.
- Use humour to make a talk entertaining and gain the attention of your audience.
- Give specific examples. Definite facts are more convincing than abstract ideas, and give the audience something to talk about if there is a question-and-answer session.
- Build up your argument starting with the least important points and working up to the most important ones.
- If you have to introduce difficult concepts, start with easier concepts and build up from there.
- However you structure your talk, it is crucial that you provide a strong, clear conclusion, reiterating your key points and touching upon any issues which may arise in future from what you have said.

Delivery

However well you have planned your presentation, it is vital that you deliver it in a clear and confident manner:

- Do not write a text and read it word-for-word. Make notes, possibly on cards, to remind yourself what you are going to say and in what sequence, and deliver your talk from those.
- Rehearse your presentation beforehand so you are confident about your material and have an idea how long it will take.
- Use the left-hand margin of your notes to mark the time you should be taking for each section. This will help you to pace your talk so that you do not run out of time.

- You can use the right-hand margin to indicate things you should be doing at certain points in your talk, such as showing a particular slide. Such reminders are an important safeguard against omitting something crucial.
- Stand up straight (but not stiffly) and do not slouch.
- Keep your hands out of your pockets. Do not use hand gestures too often, as this can be distracting. Try to keep your hands at your sides as much as you can.
- Make eye contact with your audience as much as you can. Look at all the members of the audience and not just a few people. This will encourage your audience to listen, and will help you to gauge their response.
- Try not to speak too quickly. Articulate each word clearly, without being monotonous or unnatural.
- Vary your tone of voice. Try to emphasize important words and sentences.
- Consider the volume at which you are speaking. Try not to trail away at the end of sentences. Project your voice by speaking from the chest — not the throat — and opening your mouth a bit more widely than usual.
- Try not to use too many "um"s and "er"s.
- Try not to clear your throat too often.
- Do not try to talk while the audience is laughing or applauding.
- Make a point of stopping briefly — maybe taking a sip of water — at the end of each phase of your talk. This will indicate that you have reached a natural pause, and give you a chance to compose yourself before the next part.

How do I cope with nerves?
If you are at all nervous, work out a way to relax before you speak. Breathe deeply, review your notes, and go over how you planned to begin. If you make a mistake or forget your place while you are speaking, calmly admit your mistake, and carry on as soon as you can. Whatever you do, don't panic.

Should I use audiovisual aids?

Many presentations can be made more interesting by using equipment such as film, video tapes, slides, overhead projectors, and audio tapes. However, these can also present problems. Think about the following points:

- Does your presentation really require audiovisual aids, or will these just be a distraction?
- Are the audiovisual aids you want available for your use?
- Is there enough room in the venue to set up and use the equipment?
- Are there enough power points in the venue?
- Can the room can be darkened easily?
- Will everyone be able to see and hear?
- Will you require someone to assist you in operating the equipment?

Preparing audiovisual aids

Whatever equipment you decide to use — even if it is only basic equipment such as handouts, charts, posters, or a blackboard — make sure it is thoroughly prepared. Remember:

- Do not use too many visuals. This will only cause confusion to you and your audience.
- Keep posters and slides simple. Use large, bold letters.
- Find out how many copies of any handouts you need to produce.
- Give your audience plenty of time to take in whatever you are showing them.
- Test your equipment before you use it.
- Check that any slides are clean and are fed into the projector correctly.
- Get together any spare bulbs or leads you might need.
- Try out any tapes and test sound levels before you give your presentation.

PART THREE

GUIDE TO THE ENGLISH LANGUAGE

SPELLING

Why does spelling matter?

Spelling can determine the impression you make on your examiner, prospective employer, or whoever is reading what you have written. Poor spelling will be viewed as a sign of carelessness. Conversely, good spelling will suggest that you are comfortable with the language and that you have given thought and care to your work.

Ten spelling rules worth remembering

1 Adding suffixes to words ending in 'e':

- When adding an ending beginning with a vowel to words ending with a final silent 'e', drop the final 'e'.
  plate → plated   hate → hating
- For a word ending in '-ce' or '-ge', keep the final 'e' when adding an ending beginning with 'a', 'o', or 'u' in order to preserve the soft sound.
  change → changeable   outrage → outrageous
- When adding endings to a word which ends in '-ee', keep both 'e's.
  disagree → disagreeable; disagreeing

2 Adding suffixes to words ending in 'y':

- When adding any vowel suffix except '-ing' to a word ending in the pattern *consonant+y*, change the final 'y' to 'i'.
  rely → reliable   try → tried   sky → skies

3 Adding suffixes to words ending in 'c':

- When adding an ending beginning with 'e', 'i', or 'y' to a word ending in 'c', add a 'k' to keep the hard sound.
  panic → panicking; panicky
- There is one exception worth remembering.
  arc → arced; arcing

4 Doubling final consonants:

- Double the final consonant when adding a vowel suffix to a word ending in the pattern *consonant-vowel-consonant* where the stress is on the second syllable if there is more than one syllable.
  forget → forgetting   begin → beginner
- Always double the letter 'l' if it follows a consonant+vowel, even if the syllable is unstressed.
  appal → appalled   travel → traveller
- Do not double the consonants 'h', 'w', 'x', and 'y', even if they follow the above pattern.
  box → boxes; boxing   say → saying
- When adding the ending '-es' to make a noun ending in 's' into a plural, do not double the 's'.
  gas → gases   focus → focuses

5 The endings '-ize' and '-ise':

- In Britain both '-ize' and '-ise' are acceptable. In American English '-ize' is the preferred ending for many verbs.
  emphasize or *emphasise   specialize* or *specialise*
- Some words are always spelt with '-ise', many being those where the word could not stand on its own if the ending were removed.
  *advertise   advise   chastise   despise   devise
  revise   supervise   surprise   televise*
- A few words are spelt '-yse'.
  analyse   breathalyse

6 Words ending '-ful':

- The ending '-ful' is always spelt with one 'l' when combined with another word to form an adjective or a noun.
  mouthful   painful   spoonful   useful

7 Plural endings of nouns:

- If the plural form adds an extra syllable to the noun (generally after 's', 'z', 'x', 'ch' or 'sh'), then add '-es'.
  loss → losses   box → boxes

- Most nouns ending in 'o' have the plural ending '-os'.
  cellos   curios   pianos
- Some notable exceptions have the plural ending '-oes'.
  echoes   heroes   potatoes   tomatoes
- Some nouns ending in '-f' or '-fe' form plurals by changing the 'f' to 'v' and adding '-es'.
  calf → calves   knife → knives

8 Words beginning 'ante-' and 'anti-':

- Use 'ante-' in words which mean 'before in time or position'.
  antechamber   antedate   antenatal
- Use 'anti-' in words which mean 'against' or 'opposite'.
  antibiotic   anticlimax   antisocial

9 Words beginning 'il-', 'im-', 'in-', and 'ir-':

- When words with the prefixes 'il-', 'im-', or 'ir-' have the meaning of 'not', 'in', 'into', 'towards', or 'within', spell them with double letters ('ill-', 'imm-', or 'irr-').
  illegal   immigrate   irregular
- If you can recognize what follows the prefix 'in-' as a word which can stand on its own in English, then spell it with one 'n'.
  incredible   inelegant   insincere
- If the part which follows the prefix 'in-' begins with an 'n', then spell the word with two 'n's.
  innate   innumerable

10 The 'i' before 'e' rule:

- When a syllable containing the letters 'i' and 'e' makes an 'ee' sound, then the 'i' comes before the 'e'...
  achieve   believe   niece   piece
- ...except after 'c'.
  ceiling   perceive   receive
- There are a few notable exceptions to this general rule.
  either   neither   protein   seize   weird

Words that are commonly misspelt

Here is a list of words which are frequently misspelt. You may find it helpful to practise spelling all the words in this list, or use it to pick out and practise those which you find difficult:

accommodate
address *(double d)*
aggravate
analysis
beautiful
bureaucracy
business
camouflage
committee
connoisseur
conscience
cynicism
despair
desperate
detach *(no t before c)*
disappear *(single s)*
disappoint
disastrous
discipline
dissatisfied *(double s)*
ecstasy
embarrassed
environment
euthanasia
exaggerate
excellent
excerpt *(silent p)*
extraordinary
facetious
foreign
freight
fulfil
gauge
gorgeous
government
guarantee
haemorrhage
harass *(single r)*

height
hierarchy
honorary
humorous
hygiene
hypocrisy
idiosyncrasy
illegible
independent
indict
innocuous *(double n)*
inoculate *(single n)*
instalment
integrate
intelligent
irritable
jewellery
judg(e)ment *(optional e)*
knowledge
laboratory
leukaemia
lieutenant
liquefy *(-efy not -ify)*
maintenance
manoeuvre
margarine *(two as)*
medi(a)eval *(optional a)*
mischievous
misogynist
mortgage *(silent t)*
necessary
occurred *(double r)*
parallel
parliament
perceive
permanent
phlegm
piece

playwright
possession
prejudice
privilege
professor
pronunciation
psychology
query
questionnaire
receipt
reconnaissance
refrigerator *(no d)*
sacrilege

satellite
sausage
separate
sergeant
silhouette
skilful *(no double l)*
sovereign
stupefy *(-efy not -ify)*
supersede
surprise
temperature
veterinary

Words that are often confused

The following pairs of words sound alike. Be careful not to confuse their spellings:

accept and **except**

- To **accept** something is to take or tolerate it.
- **Except** means other than or apart from.

affect and **effect**

- To **affect** something is to influence or change it, or act in that particular way.
- An **effect** is a result or impression something gives.
- To **effect** a change is to make it happen.

bought and **brought**

- **Bought** is the past tense and past participle of the verb 'to buy'.
- **Brought** is the past tense and past participle of the verb 'to bring'.

canvas and **canvass**

- **Canvas** is strong cloth.
- To **canvass** is to persuade people to vote in a particular way or to find out their opinions on a subject.

chord and **cord**

- A **chord** is a group of three or more musical notes played together.
- **Cord** is strong thick string or electrical wire.

complement and **compliment**

- A **complement** is something which goes well with another.
- To **complement** something is to go well with it.
- A **compliment** is an expression of admiration.
- To **compliment** someone is to express admiration for them.

council and **counsel**

- A **council** is a group of people elected to look after the affairs of an area.
- **Counsel** is advice; to **counsel** is to give advice.

currant and **current**

- A **currant** is a small dried grape.
- A **current** is a flow of water, air, or electricity.
- **Current** also means happening.

desert and **dessert**

- A **desert** is a region of land with little plant life.
- To **desert** someone is to abandon them.
- A **dessert** is sweet food served after the main course of a meal.

discreet and **discrete**

- If you are **discreet** you avoid causing embarrassment with private matters.
- **Discrete** means separate or distinct.

draft and draught

- A **draft** is an early rough version of a speech or document.
- A **draught** is a current of cold air or an amount of liquid you swallow.
- **Draughts** is a board game.
- A person who draws plans is a **draughtsman**.

ensure and insure

- To **ensure** something happens is to make certain it happens.
- To **insure** something is to take out cover against its loss.
- To **insure** against something is to do something in order to protect yourself or prevent it.

envelop and envelope

- To **envelop** something is to cover or surround it.
- An **envelope** is a paper covering for a letter.

flair and flare

- **Flair** is natural ability or style.
- A **flare** is a bright flame used as a signal.
- To **flare** is to suddenly burn or start up.
- To **flare** is also to spread out.

idle and idol

- If you are **idle** you are doing nothing.
- An **idol** is a famous person loved by fans or something worshipped as a god.

its and it's

- **Its** refers to something belonging or relating to things that have already been mentioned: *The lion lifted its head*.
- **It's** means "it is" or "it has": *It's cold*.

key and **quay**

- A **key** is a piece of metal that fits into a hole.
- A **quay** is a place where boats are tied up.

leant and **lent**

- **Leant** is the past tense and past participle of the verb 'to lean'.
- **Lent** is the past tense and past participle of the verb 'to lend'.

licence and **license**

- A **licence** is an official document which entitles you to carry out a particular activity.
- To **license** an activity means to give official permission for it.

lightening and **lightning**

- If something is **lightening** it is becoming less dark.
- **Lightning** is flashes of light in the sky.

loose and **lose**

- Something **loose** is not firmly held or close fitting.
- To **lose** is no longer to have something or to be beaten.

meter and **metre**

- A **meter** is a device which measures and records something.
- A **metre** is a unit of measurement.

miner, **minor**, and **mynah**

- A **miner** is a person who works in a mine.
- A **minor** is a person under the age of eighteen.
- **Minor** also means less important or serious.
- A **mynah** bird is a tropical bird which can mimic speech.

passed and past

- **Passed** is the past tense and past participle of the verb 'to pass'.
- The **past** is the period of time before the present.
- **Past** describes things which existed before the present.
- To go **past** something is to go beyond it.

personal and personnel

- **Personal** means belonging or relating to a particular person.
- **Personnel** are the people who work for an organization.

practice and practise

- **Practice** is something that people do regularly.
- A doctor's or lawyer's **practice** is his or her business.
- To **practise** is to do something regularly.

precede and proceed

- Something which **precedes** another happens before it.
- If you **proceed** you start or continue to do something.

prescribe and proscribe

- A doctor **prescribes** treatment.
- To **proscribe** something is to ban or forbid it.

principal and principle

- **Principal** means main or most important.
- The **principal** of a school or college is the person in charge.
- A **principle** is a belief you have about the way you should behave, or a general rule or scientific law.

rain, rein, and reign

- **Rain** is water falling from the clouds.
- **Reins** are straps which control a horse.
- To **reign** is to rule a country or be a noticeable feature of a situation.

sceptic and septic

- A **sceptic** is someone who has doubts about things that other people believe.
- If a wound becomes **septic**, it becomes infected with poison.

stationary and stationery

- **Stationary** means not moving.
- **Stationery** is paper, pens, and other writing equipment.

straight and strait

- **Straight** means continuing in the same direction, or level.
- A **strait** is a narrow strip of sea.
- If someone is in a bad situation, they are in difficult **straits**.

their, there, and they're

- **Their** refers to something belonging or relating to people or things which have already been mentioned: *It was their fault.*
- **There** means at that place: *She is sitting over there.*
- **They're** means "they are": *They're very angry.*

waist and waste

- Your **waist** is the middle part of your body.
- If you **waste** something, you use too much of it on something that isn't important.

wander and wonder

- If you **wander** around a place, you walk around in a casual way.
- If you **wonder** about something you think about it with curiosity.
- If you **wonder** at something, you are surprised or amazed at it.

whose and **who's**

- You use **whose** to ask to whom something belongs, or at the beginning of a clause which gives information about something relating or belonging to the thing or person you have just mentioned: *Whose gun is this?*
- **Who's** means "who is" or "who has": *Who's at the door?*

your and **you're**

- **Your** means belonging or relating to the person or group of people that someone is speaking to, or shows that something belongs or relates to people in general: *Your driving ability is affected by just one or two drinks.*
- **You're** means "you are": *You're kidding!*

How can I improve my spelling?

- Use mnemonics to remember words which you find difficult to spell. If you do not know of one which already exists for a particular word, try making up your own. Here are a few examples:
  environment — there is <u>iron</u> in the envi<u>ron</u>ment
  necessary — you have one <u>c</u>ollar and two <u>s</u>ocks
  stationery — <u>e</u>nvelopes are station<u>e</u>ry
- Write out a problem word a number of times until you feel you can do it automatically.
- Carefully pronounce a word out loud or in your head, exaggerating the pronunciation, and including any silent letters.
- Visualize the word in your head, trying to remember the letters and its shape.
- Break the word down into syllables, and learn each part separately.
- Make a habit of looking up in a dictionary any words you are doubtful about.

GRAMMAR

Key terms explained

It is not necessary to learn a lot of complicated grammatical rules to write good English. However, you may find it useful to understand these terms:

- **Active:** a form of a verb used to indicate that the subject is performing the action; for example *broke* in *He broke the window*. Compare **passive**.
- **Adjective:** a word that adds information about a noun or pronoun; for example *large* in *a large cat*.
- **Adverb:** a word that modifies a sentence, verb, adverb, or adjective; for example *easily*, *very*, and *happily* in *They could easily envy the very happily married couple*.
- **Article:** See **definite article; indefinite article**.
- **Clause:** a group of words, consisting of a subject and a predicate including a verb, that does not necessarily make a complete sentence.
- **Compound:** a form produced by combining two or more existing words.
- **Conjunction:** a word that connects words, phrases, or clauses; for example *and*, *if*, and *but*.
- **Definite article:** the word *the*. Compare **indefinite article**.
- **Indefinite article:** either of the words *a* or *an*. Compare **definite article**.
- **Infinitive:** a form of the verb which is used without a particular subject; in English, the infinitive usually consists of the word *to* followed by the verb.
- **Interjection:** a word or phrase which is used on its own and expresses sudden emotion; for example *ouch*.
- **Intransitive verb:** a verb that does not take an object; for example *to faint*. Compare **transitive verb**.
- **Modifier:** a word or phrase that makes the sense of another word more specific; for example *garage* is a modifier of *door* in *garage door*.
- **Noun:** a word that refers to a person, place, or thing; for example *Vera*, *Peru*, and *carrot*.

- **Object:** a noun that receives the action of a verb; for example *the bottle* in *She threw the bottle*.
- **Participle:** a form of a verb that is used in compound tenses or as an adjective; for example *eaten*, *gone*, and *running*.
- **Passive:** a form of a verb used to indicate that the subject is the recipient of the action; for example *was broken* in *The window was broken by a stone*. Compare **active**.
- **Phrasal verb:** a phrase that consists of a verb plus an adverb or preposition; for example *take in*.
- **Phrase:** a group of words forming a unit of meaning in a sentence.
- **Predicate:** the part of a sentence in which something is said about the subject; for example *catches mice* in the sentence *The cat catches mice*.
- **Preposition:** a word used before a noun or pronoun to relate it to other words; for example *in* in *He is in the car*.
- **Pronoun:** a word, such as *she* or *it*, that replaces a noun that has already been or is about to be mentioned.
- **Sentence:** a sequence of words constituting a statement, question, or a command.
- **Subject:** a word or phrase that represents the person or thing performing the action of the verb in a sentence; for example *the cat* in the sentence *The cat catches mice*.
- **Tense:** the form of a verb that indicates whether the action referred to in the sentence is located in the past, the present, or the future; *ate* is the past tense of *to eat*.
- **Transitive verb:** a verb that requires an object; for example *to find*. Compare **intransitive verb**.
- **Verb:** a word that is used to indicate the occurrence or performance of an action or the existence of a state; for example *run*, *make*, or *do*.

Common grammatical problems

Here are some common grammatical problems to watch out for in your writing:

- **Double negatives:** Two negative forms make a positive. Avoid using a sentence like *There isn't no food in the fridge* if what you are trying to say is that the fridge has no food in it.
- **Confusing the past tense and the past participle:** Many irregular verbs use different forms for the past tense and the past participle. The past tense stands on its own (for example *rang*), whereas the past participle is used with other words to form compound tenses (for example *has rung*).
- **'Shall' and 'will':** You do not need to follow the old rule that *shall* is used with *I* and *we* and *will* with *you*, *he*, *she*, *it*, and *they* to express the future tense. Either is acceptable, although *shall* is now less common than *will*.
- **Agreement:** If the subject of a sentence is singular, use a singular verb; if the subject is plural, use a plural verb. Make the subject and verb agree regardless of any phrases or clauses coming between them. If two or more subjects are joined by *and*, use a plural verb: *A notebook and pen are all I need*. A collective noun such as *family* or *team* usually takes a singular verb, even though it refers to more than one thing.
- **Consistency of tenses:** Do not shift verb tenses – for example, between the past and the present – without reason.
- **Comparatives and superlatives:** The endings *-er* and *-est* can be added to most shorter adjectives to change the meaning: *My bed is hard; your bed is harder; his is the hardest*. Most long adjectives and most adverbs use *more* and *most* (or *less* and *least*) instead of *-er* and *-est*: *My house is beautiful; your house is more beautiful; his is the most beautiful*. Do not combine the two ways of expressing comparatives and superlatives – avoid phrases such as *more faster*.
- **Illogical comparisons:** Do not make comparisons involving adjectives such as *empty*, *dead*, *unique*, and *perfect*. A thing is either unique or not unique; there are no degrees of uniqueness.

- **Ambiguity:** Make sure that a sentence cannot have two meanings. A common source of ambiguity is a pronoun that might refer to two different nouns. For example, in the sentence *Mr White has given the job to Richard because he knows what has to be done* it is unclear whether *he* refers to Mr White or to Richard. In such cases you should reword the sentence to make your meaning clear: *Mr White has given the job to Richard, who knows what has to be done*.
- **Non-sentences:** Do not punctuate a fragment of a sentence, such as a phrase or clause, as if it were a complete sentence. Each sentence must have a subject and a verb which says something about the subject.
- **Comma splices:** Do not use a comma to join two clauses if each is capable of standing as a sentence in its own right. Join the two clauses with a semicolon, or by using a conjunction: *Our team won easily; it had a better coach* or *Our team won easily because it had a better coach*.
- **Word order:** Be careful about where you place the adverbs *almost*, *only*, *nearly*, *scarcely*, *hardly*, *just*, and *even*. These words should stand next to the words they modify.
- **Ending with a preposition:** Avoid ending a sentence with a preposition unless the sentence would otherwise sound awkward.
- **Split infinitives:** The two parts of an infinitive belong together. Adverbs which modify the infinitive should be placed either before or after, but not in between the two parts; for example *I asked her to call occasionally* is preferable to *I asked her to occasionally call*.
- **Dangling modifiers:** A modifier 'dangles' when there is no word in the sentence that it can sensibly modify. For example, in the sentence *Flying over Switzerland, the jagged Alps appeared awesome* there is no word to which *flying* can sensibly refer. The sentence seems to say that the Alps were flying. In such cases, you should reword the sentence to indicate the thing to which the modifier refers: *As we flew over Switzerland, the jagged Alps appeared awesome*.

You can find out more about grammar in *Collins Gem English Grammar* by Ronald G. Hardie (HarperCollins, 1990).

PUNCTUATION

Punctuation is an essential part of written English. If you are aware of the variety of punctuation available, you will find it easier to express exactly what you mean. On the other hand, if you use punctuation incorrectly, you can sometimes end up writing the opposite of what you intend to say. Consider the difference between these sentences:

After eating, my brother John had a cup of tea.
After eating my brother, John had a cup of tea.

The incorrect position of the comma in the second sentence makes it seem that John is a cannibal. To avoid such errors, you should be aware of the correct uses of the different punctuation marks.

Full stop (.)

- The full stop is used to mark the end of any sentence which is not a question or exclamation.
  Your grant cheque has arrived.
- It is also used after an abbreviation or initial.
  op. cit.   Prof. West   J.R. Hartley
- Use a full stop after an expression that stands by itself but is not a complete sentence.
  Good morning.

Question mark (?)

- The question mark is used to mark the end of a question.
  Has my grant cheque arrived?

- Note that after an indirect question or a polite request, a full stop is used rather than a question mark.
  Cathy asked whether the cheque had arrived.
  Will you please send me an application form.

Exclamation mark (!)

- The exclamation mark is used after emphatic expressions and exclamations.
  I can't believe it!
- The exclamation mark quickly loses its effect if it is used too much. After a sentence expressing mild excitement or humour, it is better to use a full stop.
  It is a beautiful day.

Comma (,)

- The comma indicates a short pause between different elements within a sentence. This happens, for example, when a sentence consists of two main clauses joined by a conjunction.
  My mouth opened, but no words came out.
- A comma may also separate an introductory phrase or clause from the main clause in a sentence.
  After 18 months at LSE, I gave it up and did mathematics at York.
- However, a short introductory phrase does not need to be followed by a comma.
  After lunch the lectures were equally compelling.
- A comma is also used to indicate that a series of words is not part of the main flow of thought in a sentence and is not essential to the meaning.
  The company, which was formed in 1981, makes office furniture.
- However, where a phrase is an essential part of the main sentence, it is not marked off by commas.
  Women who smoke are more likely to suffer a heart attack.
- When words such as 'therefore', 'however', and 'moreover' are inserted into a sentence to show how a

train of thought is progressing, they should be marked off by commas.

We are confident, however, that the case will be successful.

- The comma is also used to separate items in a list or series.

  I would make this soup with carrots, leeks, and potatoes.

- Commas are used to separate the name of a person or people being addressed from the rest of the sentence.

  Thank you, ladies and gentlemen, for your cooperation.

- The comma is also used to separate words in quotation marks from the rest of the sentence.

  "I'm reporting you to the manager," she cried.

- You can also use a comma to indicate a break in sense between two words when there might otherwise be a doubt about the meaning.

  Inside, the house was a complete mess.

Colon (:)

- The colon is used to introduce a list.

  There are three kinds of lie: lies, damned lies, and statistics.

- The colon is also used to introduce a quotation.

  As Voltaire said: "The art of medicine consists of amusing the patient while nature cures the disease."

- The colon can also be used to introduce an explanation of a statement.

  Your editorial pinpoints the reason for the plight of the arts: failure to increase seat prices.

Semicolon (;)

- The semicolon is stronger than a comma, but weaker than a full stop. It is used to mark the break between two main clauses, especially where there is balance or contrast between them.

  I'm not that interested in acid house myself; I prefer Indie music.

- The semicolon is also used instead of a comma to separate clauses or items in a long list when there are commas within the clauses or listed items.

He was back in hospital twice: firstly, with bruises on his forearms after being beaten up; secondly, to have five stitches put in a gash on his hand.

Apostrophe (')

- The apostrophe is used to indicate possession. It is usually added to the end of a word and followed by an 's'.
  Craig's book   children's programmes
- If a plural word already ends in 's', the apostrophe follows that letter.
  my parents' generation   seven years' bad luck
- Do not use an apostrophe to form plurals.
  a pound of tomatoes [not _tomato's_]
- It is acceptable to add an apostrophe to form the plural of a number, letter, or symbol.
  P's and Q's   7's   £'s
- Do not use an apostrophe to form possessive pronouns.
  I happen to be a fan of hers. [not _her's_]
- The apostrophe is also used to show that a letter or letters have been omitted.
  rock'n'roll   Who's next?   five o'clock

Quotation marks (" ") (' ')

- Quotation marks, also called inverted commas, are used to mark the beginning and end of a speaker's exact words or thoughts.
  "I'm impressed," said Tweed.
  "Was this guy a fisherman?" I wondered.
- Quotation marks are not used when a speaker's words are reported indirectly rather than in their exact form.
  Tweed said that he was impressed.
  I wondered if this guy was a fisherman.
- Quotation marks can also be used to indicate the title of a book, piece of music, etc.

They met again at a gala performance of "The Magic Flute".

- Quotation marks are also used to draw attention to the fact that a word or phrase is being used in an unusual way, or that a word itself is the subject of discussion.

  Braille allows a blind person to 'see' with the fingers.

  What rhymes with 'orange'?

Hyphen (-)

- Certain words that are formed from two separate parts are spelt with a hyphen.

  great-grandmother   self-conscious   forty-two

- A hyphen is often used when there would otherwise be an awkward combination of letters, or confusion with another word.

  Peron was re-elected president.

  He was asked to re-cover family bibles.

- The modern trend is to omit the hyphen in compound forms provided there is no ambiguity or awkward combination of letters.

  antiterrorist   nonmedical

- The hyphen is used to join two words which are combined to act as an adjective.

  She adopted a no-nonsense approach.

- The hyphen is also used to divide a word that will not fit at the end of a printed line.

Dash (—)

- The dash is used to mark an abrupt change in the flow of a sentence, either showing a sudden change of subject, or marking off incidental information.

  I'm not sure — what was the question again?

  The furnishing is a little – how shall we say — extravagant.

- The dash can also be used to indicate that a speech has been cut off abruptly.

  "Go ahead and —" He broke off as Andrei seized his arm.

Brackets ( ) [ ]

- Brackets are used to enclose incidental material that has been inserted into the text. In formal writing this sort of material is usually marked off with commas or dashes, and brackets are reserved for giving references or translations of foreign phrases.
  The role of sodium is discussed fully in Chapter 7 (see page 137).
  "La Ardilla Roja" (The Red Squirrel) is a flashy trick-box of a film.

- Square brackets are used to enclose remarks and explanations which are not part of the original sentence, but are inserted by an author when making a quotation.
  Jackson said, "I think that five million [dollars] should do it."

Ellipsis (...)

- Ellipsis is a sequence of three dots used to indicate that some words have been omitted from a quotation.
  The inspector reported that the kitchen was "dirty...infested with insects...and generally unfit for use".

- Ellipsis is also used to indicate a pause or hesitation.
  He was...er...rather drunk, I'm afraid.

USAGE

Using English appropriately

Using words carelessly or inaccurately can cause irritation and offence. Try to avoid these general faults:

- **Slang:** Slang is a very informal part of language used in speech by people who want to avoid solemn or pompous language. It is not appropriate for written work and formal talks.

- **Jargon and buzz words:** Jargon is the technical language of a group of specialists. A buzz word is a slang technical word, often used by people to show that they are in the know about a certain subject. Avoid using these in written work. Think of your reader as intelligent but uninformed about the subject on which you are writing.

- **Clichés:** A cliché is a phrase or expression, such as *leave no stone unturned* or *at this moment in time*, that has been used so often that it has lost its power to surprise or inform the reader. Avoid such overused expressions.

- **Offensive language:** Careless or inaccurate language can reinforce stereotypes and promote negative attitudes to certain groups of people. You should beware of using terms which may cause offence to your readers. Some writers have attempted to establish 'politically correct' language, which avoids prejudice of any kind. However, this language can seem unnatural and ridiculous when taken to extremes.

- **Sexism:** Sexism in language is not always obvious because distinctions based on gender are part of the structure of many languages. Avoid sexist language and usage, or you risk alienating and offending half your readers. Use neutral terms like *poet, manager,* and *author* rather than gender-specific terms like *poetess, manageress,* and *authoress*. Use the phrase *he or she* or plural pronouns (*they, their, them*) rather than male pronouns (*he, his, him*) when you refer to both sexes.

Words that are commonly misused

Here is a list of words and phrases which are often used incorrectly. Be careful when you use these:

- **aggravate:** Strictly, this means 'to make worse': *He aggravated a cartilage injury.* It is now often used to mean 'annoy' or 'irritate', but some people still object to this usage in formal English.

- **among:** *Among* is used when three or more choices or possibilities are concerned: *The prize money was divided among the four winners.* Use *between* when there are only two choices.
- **amoral:** Do not confuse *amoral* with *immoral*. *Immoral* is used of anything that breaks moral rules: *Most societies consider it immoral to own human slaves.* You should use *amoral* only when you are referring to something to which morality is irrelevant, or to people who have no moral code: *In the amoral world of animals there are no murders.*
- **between:** *Between* is used when there are only two choices or possibilities concerned: *This is just between the two of us.* Use *among* when there are three or more choices.
- **biannual:** If an event is biannual, it happens twice a year. A biennial event happens once every two years.
- **chairman:** Many people feel that *chairman* is too suggestive of the dominance of men in positions of authority. *Chairperson* or *chair* can be used instead, or use *president* if you prefer.
- **chronic:** *Chronic* means 'lasting over a long time' or 'constantly recurring': *chronic alcoholism.* The use of *chronic* to mean 'bad' or 'serious' should be avoided except in informal situations.
- **contagious:** A contagious disease is passed on by contact of some sort. An infectious disease is passed on without personal contact.
- **decimate:** The original meaning of this verb was 'destroy one in ten'. The extended meaning of 'destroy or kill a large proportion of' is now more common than the original: *A species of white fly decimated lettuce, melon, and other crops.*
- **dilemma:** Strictly, a dilemma is a choice between two courses of action, neither of which is entirely acceptable. It is better to use *problem* if the situation does not involve that element of choice.
- **disinterested:** Do not confuse *disinterested* with *uninterested*. *Disinterested* means 'impartial' or

'unbiased': *You will be a disinterested adviser.* The adjective meaning 'showing or feeling a lack of interest' is *uninterested*: *London publishers were uninterested in Scottish literature.*

- **electronic:** *Electronic* is used to refer to equipment like television sets and computers, in which current is controlled by transistors and valves. *Electrical* is used in a more general sense, often to refer to the use of electricity as opposed to other forms of energy: *an electrical appliance. Electric* is often restricted to the description of devices or to concepts relating to the flow of current: *electric fire. Electric* and *electrical* are often used interchangeably.

- **empathy:** If you have sympathy for someone, you have feeling for them, especially if they are in difficult circumstances. If you have empathy for them, you enter into and share their feeling.

- **enervate:** *Enervate* means 'drain' or 'weaken': *the enervating effects of the African climate.* Do not confuse it with *energize,* meaning 'invigorate' or 'give energy to'.

- **farther:** Use *farther* and *farthest* when you are referring to a literal distance: *a little farther down the road.* For figurative senses, use *further* and *furthest*: *Nothing could be further from the truth.*

- **fewer:** Do not confuse *fewer* and *less. Less* refers to quantity and not to number: *There is less water than before. Fewer* means 'smaller in number': *fewer than ten items.*

- **hang:** The normal past tense and past participle of *hang* is *hung*: *The picture was hung from a nail.* If you are talking about capital punishment or suicide, the form is *hanged*: *He hanged himself in prison.*

- **hypercritical:** If you are hypercritical, you find fault too readily; but if you are hypocritical, you pretend to be something which you are not, or behave falsely, in order to deceive someone else.

- **i.e.:** When you want to say something more specific just after talking about a subject generally, use *i.e.,* which is an abbreviation of a Latin phrase meaning 'that is to say': *at the end of each key stage, i.e. at the ages of 7, 11, 14, and 16*. The abbreviation *e.g.* is used when you are giving one or more examples of what you are talking about: *raw vegetables, e.g. carrots, celery, red and green peppers*. Do not treat these abbreviations as if they were interchangeable.

- **in case:** Always write *in case* as two words: *She was embarrassed in case someone saw them.*
- **inflammable:** The words *flammable* and *inflammable* both mean 'liable to catch fire'. *Flammable* is often preferred for warning labels as it is less likely to be misunderstood. The word meaning 'not flammable' is *nonflammable*.
- **lay:** The verbs *lay* and *lie* are often confused. *Lay* is used with an object: *The soldier laid down his arms*. *Lie* does not take an object: *I'm going to lie down*. The past tense of *lie* is spelt *lay*: *I lay down on the bed and went to sleep*. The past tense of *lay* is *laid*: *I laid the table for six*.
- **literally:** Use *literally* carefully. It can be used informally to add emphasis without adding to the meaning: *The house was literally only five minutes walk away*. The basic meaning of *literally* is 'actually'. If you use *literally* with a figure of speech, the result can be absurd: *He literally swept me off my feet*.
- **media:** *Media* is a shorthand way of referring to the various forms of mass communication. *Media* is the plural form of *medium*. Although *media* is often used as a singular noun, use it as a plural in formal contexts: *The media are quick to jump on any sign of potential disaster*.
- **momentary:** Something momentary lasts for a moment only or is temporary: *a momentary silence*. In British English the adverb *momentarily* is used of an action that takes place for a very brief time: *He paused momentarily*. In American English *momentarily* can be used of an action that is about to happen in a moment: *This plane will be landing momentarily*.

- **panacea:** A panacea is a supposed cure for all ills. It does not mean a cure for an individual problem.
- **protagonist:** Originally a protagonist was the main character in a play. It is now often used to mean 'someone who is a leading supporter of a cause'. Some people object to this new usage and avoid it by using *proponent* or *advocate*. Do not confuse *protagonist* with *antagonist*, which means 'a person who is hostile to you'.
- **quote:** The verb *quote* means 'use the exact words of another person'. *Quote* is often used as a noun, but it is better to avoid this in formal writing and use *quotation* instead.
- **re:** *Re* is used in business or official correspondence to mean 'with reference to': *Re your letter, your remarks have been noted*. Avoid using *re* in general English. Use *with reference to*, *about*, or *concerning* instead.
- **refute:** Do not use *refute* when you mean *deny*. They are are not synonyms. If you deny something, you state that it is not true. If you refute it, you gather evidence in order to prove that it is not true: *All he could do was deny the allegations since he was unable to refute them.*
- **subsequent:** When one thing is subsequent to another, it follows on in time. When one thing is consequent on another, it happens as a result of the first event.
- **try:** You can use *try* with *to* before another verb: *I will try to do my best*. The construction *try and* is informal and is better restricted to spoken usage.
- **unexceptional:** If something is unexceptional it is no better than you would expect: *a pretty unexceptional bunch of players*. If a statement or someone's behaviour is unexceptionable there is no possible objection that can be made about it: *a man of unexceptionable character*.

- **whom:** In formal and written contexts use *whom* when the object form of *who* is required. In informal contexts, you can use *who*, especially near the beginning of a sentence: *Who were you looking for?* Also use *whom* where it closely follows a preposition: *To whom did you give it?*

You can find out more about correct and effective use of English in *Collins Gem Dictionary of English Usage* by Ronald G. Hardie (HarperCollins, 1991).

PART FOUR

GUIDE TO JOB SEEKING

FINDING THE JOB YOU WANT

Your College Careers Service

You can get information and advice about which jobs are available from the Careers Advisory Service at your university or college. Keep an eye on notice boards or ask the staff for help. In many institutions you can continue to use the Careers Service for up to three years after completing your course.

How can the Careers Service help?

The Careers Service offers a variety of services:

- Help in identifying the most suitable career for you.
- Information and advice on where to apply for jobs.
- Help on how to apply for jobs.
- Seminars and courses on a wide range of subjects designed to give an insight into the world of work.
- Lists of job vacancies for students who are available for immediate employment.
- Job fairs at which a number of companies set up stalls and give out information about employment opportunities.
- 'Milk-round' visits at which companies interview candidates.

Why should I bother using the Careers Service?

- It is free.
- The staff of the Careers Service are experts who are used to helping people in your position.
- The Careers Service probably has good contacts with potential employers.

Where else can I find out about jobs?

Your Careers Service is likely to be your main source of information. However, you may also find out about jobs from other places:

- Talk to your course tutor. Your tutor may have useful contacts, especially if you are on a vocational course. Even if you are on a nonvocational course, your tutor will know what jobs people on your course have found in the past.
- Use your personal contacts. Friends and relations may give you an idea about what is available and what you would like to do.
- Look in local and national newspapers. Many newspapers advertise jobs in certain areas (for example, education, law, computing) on specific days. Get to know which papers have the jobs that interest you on which days.

PREPARING A CURRICULUM VITAE

What is a curriculum vitae?

A curriculum vitae (usually shortened to 'CV') is a record of your educational qualifications, work experience, interests, skills, and personal details. It is sent to a prospective employer together with a covering letter or an application form when you apply for a job. Your CV creates the vital first impression of you with your prospective employer, so you should take great care when you prepare it. Keep a copy of your CV so that it can be easily updated and adapted for your next application.

What should I put in my CV?

There are various ways of setting out a CV. The standard way is to give information in blocks under the following headings:

- **Personal details:** Give your full name, address and contact numbers, including postcodes and dialling codes. If you have a home address and a term-time address, give both and label them clearly so that the employer knows how to get hold of you at any time.

You may also give your date of birth, sex, nationality and marital status, although there is no need to give this information, especially if you think it may lead to discrimination against you.

- **Statement of objectives:** This is a short paragraph, normally of no more than one or two sentences, in which you state your aim in making the application.
- **Education:** Give the names and locations of schools and colleges you have attended, with dates of attendance. List the qualifications you gained, including grades for the latest qualifications. Give an indication of qualifications you expect to gain at the end of your course. If your academic record is not as good as it might be, shuffle the order of your CV so that the stronger sections come before this one.
- **Vocational training and qualifications:** List any other training courses you have attended and qualifications gained. Give the name of the course together with the dates you attended and the name of the training body.
- **Work experience:** List any jobs you have had (including casual, part-time, and voluntary work) either in chronological order or starting with the most recent and working back. Give the employer's name and location, dates of employment, the employer's business (if this not obvious), your position, and also a short description of your responsibilities.
- **Skills:** Include such skills as driving, typing and shorthand speeds, foreign languages of which you have a working knowledge or in which you are fluent, knowledge of computer software, and so on.
- **Personal interests:** List three or four activities you do in your spare time, such as a certain kind of sport or a certain form of cooking.
- **Referees:** Give the names and addresses of two people who have agreed to act as referees. One referee should be your course tutor or someone who has taught you at college. It is a good idea to give a recent employer, or someone who has direct experience of you at work

as your second referee. Before you put their names forward, you should check that your referees feel able to give you a good reference.

However, there are other ways of laying out a CV. You should arrange the information in whichever way presents you most favourably. Look at the CVs on pages 106 and 107 and decide which format would be most appropriate for you.

Tips for a winning CV

- Use a good typewriter or word processor.
- Use good quality white paper.
- Send an individually prepared document rather than a photocopied CV.
- Check your spelling thoroughly, using a dictionary where necessary. Do not rely on a computer spell-checker to correct your spelling.
- Never send out a CV unless it has been read by at least one person other than yourself.
- Use headings highlighted in bold or underlined to mark the different sections of your CV.
- Use lists. These are quicker to read and easier to take in than paragraphs of full sentences. They can also help avoid tedious repetition of the word 'I'.
- Do not try to say too much. You can expand on important points at other stages of the application process. Your CV should not exceed two pages.
- Do not include information that is not relevant to the job for which you are applying.
- Employers will not usually be interested in your education before the age of twelve.
- Do not include unnecessary information that will give an unfavourable impression of yourself.
- Make sure that all the information in your CV is up to date.

CURRICULUM VITAE

Personal Details:

Name:	Stuart Dent
Address:	29 College Road
	Newtown NT1 2AB
Telephone:	(01998) 3334455

Objective:

To gain a position in environmental management where I can acquire the necessary skills and experience to become a wildlife park warden.

Education:

1987-1992:	Newtown High School
	Eight GCSE passes
1992-1994:	Newtown Sixth Form College
	'A' levels: Biology (B), Geography (C),
	Business Studies (D)
1995-1998:	University of Newtown
	B.Sc. in Environmental Biology
	(expecting to graduate in July 1998)

Work Experience:

1994-1995:	Oldborough Wildlife Park
	Voluntary Helper: Assisted with surveys and
	general duties
1996:	Oldborough Wildlife Park
	Assistant Warden: Organized surveys and
	supervised volunteers

Skills:

Leadership and man-management skills acquired during work experience
Knowledge of several computer systems and word-processing packages
Working knowledge of German

Interests:

Member of Newtown Ornithological Society
Treasurer of University of Newtown Real Ale Society
Member of University of Newtown Fencing Club

Referees:

Dr A. Smith	Mrs B. Jones
Department of Biology	Senior Warden
University of Newtown	Oldborough Wildlife Park
Newtown NT1 9CD	Oldborough OB3 8EF

Curriculum Vitae

SUSAN DENT

ADDRESS: 29 College Road, Newtown NT1 2AB

TELEPHONE: (01998) 3334455

PERSONAL PROFILE: A well-organized and highly motivated person with proven leadership skills, eager to make a career in management. Has shown aptitude for this by achieving Newtown Chamber of Commerce Gold Award for Young Entrepreneurs while a member of the Newtown Youth Enterprise Group.

SKILLS: Knowledge of several computer systems and software packages
Keyboard skills (Typing speed 80 wpm)
Full driving licence

EDUCATION AND QUALIFICATIONS:

1987-92	Newtown High School 9 GCSEs
1992-4	Newtown Sixth Form College 3 A levels: Business Studies (A), Mathematics (D), Geography (D)
1994-7	Newtown Business College Bachelor of Commerce Degree (expecting to graduate in 1997)

INTERESTS: Tennis (captained Newtown Tennis Club to district championship)
Reading American literature
Car maintenance

REFEREES:

Mr C. Browne	Mrs D. Sharma
Lecturer	Newtown Chamber of Commerce
Newtown Business College	Main Street
Newtown	Newtown
NT2 5KL	NT1 1MN

- Make sure that all periods of your life are accounted for, even if you have been unemployed. Employers will be suspicious of blank periods.
- Write about any periods of unemployment in a positive way, saying what skills you developed and how you went about seeking work.
- If appropriate, adjust some of the details of your CV to match the requirements of the job for which you are applying. You might want to stress different interests, or use a different referee for certain jobs.
- Use active and positive words to describe what you have done and can do, but avoid clichés.

WRITING LETTERS OF APPLICATION

Include a covering letter when sending your CV or application form to an employer. This should say why you are applying and point out the merits of your application.

What should I write in my covering letter?
You can use the following standard structure:

- **Sender's address:** Give your full address on the top right corner of the page. Include postcode, telephone, and other contact details, such as e-mail or fax.
- **Date:** Write the date on the left-hand side of the page. Make sure that you are writing on the day of the advertisement if possible. If you are writing only a day or two after the advertisement date, give that date anyway. If you give a later date, you may seem less than totally committed to the job.
- **Recipient's name and address:** Put the name, position, and address of the person to whom you are writing on the left-hand side, below the date.
- **Greeting:** Start the letter with *Dear Ms...*, *Dear Mr...*, *Dear Sir*, or *Dear Madam*, as appropriate. Never use a person's first name in your greeting unless this is all

you are given in the advertisement and you are unsure about their sex.

- **First paragraph:** Introduce your application by saying where you saw the advertisement or heard of the vacancy. Say that you would like to apply and are enclosing your CV (or, if appropriate, application form). Give the title of the job (copied from the advertisement) and any reference.
- **Second paragraph:** Use the next paragraph to point out any experience and skills that you have which seem particularly relevant to the advertised job. If possible, use the exact words from the advertisement and confirm that you have the qualities required. If necessary, show how you would compensate for any apparent shortcomings in your application.
- **Third paragraph:** Round off your letter by asking politely and confidently for an interview.
- **Ending:** Close the letter with *Yours sincerely* only if you greeted the person by name (e.g. *Dear Ms Jones*). If you used *Dear Sir* or *Dear Madam*, close the letter with *Yours faithfully*.
- **Signature:** Sign the letter using your normal signature. If your signature is illegible, print or write your name in capital letters underneath. Add the letters 'Encs.' to show that you are enclosing other sheets with your covering letter (or 'Enc.' if there is a single sheet enclosed).

Tips for success

- Keep it short. Selectors do not have time to read long rambling letters, and will probably be irritated by them.
- Humour can sometimes work, but it can also backfire. Do not try to use it unless you are very confident that it will be appreciated by the selector.
- If you need to write more than one side, use two sheets of paper rather than writing on the reverse of your letter.

29 College Road
Newtown NT1 2AB
(01998) 3334455

20 February 1997

Ms V Jones
Personnel Manager
The Very Large Company Ltd
Large Industrial Estate
Newtown NT6 7GH

Dear Ms Jones,

I would like to apply for the position of trainee
manager advertised in today's *Morning Post*
(reference VLC/97/01). I enclose my curriculum
vitae as requested.

I am in the final year of a Management Studies
course at Newtown Business College, and am
currently writing a report on management problems
associated with large companies on large industrial
estates. I feel that the work I have done for this
project will equip me well for the post. I have
also gained useful relevant experience during work
placements with large companies during my course.
Furthermore, I believe that I have the skills of
organization and leadership necessary to make a
success of this job: I have demonstrated these
skills in my achievements as captain of Newtown
Tennis Club and secretary of the Newtown Youth
Enterprise Group.

I hope that you consider my application suitable,
and look forward to arranging to meet you.

Yours sincerely,

Sue Dent

Enc.

- Write the letter by hand, particularly if the job advertisement requests you to.
- When copying out the name and position of the recipient, copy these exactly from the advertisement. Check the spelling carefully, as many people take mistakes in the spelling of their name or the wording of their job title as a personal insult.
- Take care to close with the appropriate form of words.
- Your application must be spotless, so take the time to make it count. Do not allow the letter to go out with blots, alterations, or crossings out. Do not use liquid paper.
- Keep a copy of the letter, so that you can remind yourself what you wrote before going to an interview.

FILLING OUT APPLICATION FORMS

On many occasions you will be asked to fill out an application form for a job. This ensures that all applicants give the same information in the same order.

Requesting a form

To get hold of an application form you may need to make a phone call or write a letter.

- If you have to phone an answering machine, speak clearly and spell any names that might give trouble. Make sure you have all the necessary information, including the reference number for the job if there is one, before you dial.
- If you write off for a form, observe the rules for covering letters (see pages 108-9). Keep this letter to one paragraph if you can. Check the spelling. Enclose a stamped, self-addressed envelope if requested. Put a first-class stamp on both envelopes.

Completing a form

Don't rush to complete the form before you have worked out exactly what you want to say. Follow these steps:

- Study carefully all the information you have received about the job. This includes the original advertisement and any information that was sent with the application form.
- Read the form from start to finish. Note any instructions and follow them to the letter.
- Look at how much space is allocated to each question. Work out from this which parts of the form are most important.
- Work out what kind of person the employer is looking for and make sure your application shows that you fit the bill.
- Before filling in the actual form, make two drafts of your application, the first on ordinary paper, and the second on a photocopy of the form. This allows you to be sure you can put everything you want to say in the space provided.
- Only now should you fill in the form, answering all the questions and using all the space provided. Use black ink as the employer will probably want to photocopy the form.
- If a particular section does not apply to you, write *N/A* to show that it is not applicable. Do not leave any sections blank.

How do I approach the questions on the form?

Questions that require straightforward factual answers do not present a problem. However many candidates do badly at the more open-ended questions on application forms. Try to answer these questions as if you were writing a covering letter:

- Show in what ways your experience matches the job description.
- Say what it is that makes you interested in the job.
- Show that your skills will be useful to the employer.

- Remember that what you write may well be used as the basis for questions in an interview. Make sure you can handle any questions that might arise from your answers.

Tips for success

- If an advertisement asks you to send for a form and fill it in, you should do exactly that. Do not send your CV with a covering letter instead, and do not return the application form incomplete with the words *see CV attached* written across it.
- Make sure your writing is neither too cramped nor too large.
- If you are an accomplished typist you may like to type your application. However, watch out for instructions saying you must fill in the form by hand.
- Keep a copy of your completed application form. You will then be able to refresh your memory about what you said in the form before an interview.
- You may find it useful to refer to any old application forms you have kept. Do not, however, simply copy answers from one form over to another.
- Add extra sheets only if this is suggested on the form itself.
- It may sometimes be worth including your CV in addition to the completed application form, particularly if you feel that it highlights strengths and experience you have not been given space to mention in the form.
- Staple any attachments to the form to stop them becoming separated.

INTERVIEWS

After the selectors have looked at all the applications for a job, they will usually draw up a short list of candidates for interview.

How should I prepare for a job interview?

Preparation is the key to successful job interviews. You will approach the interview with a lot more confidence if you are well prepared:

- Gather as much intelligence as you can about the job, the company, and the person who is likely to interview you. Your Careers Service may keep files on large employers.
- If you are not confident about handling an interview, ask your Careers Service to arrange a mock interview. You may get some interesting feedback as a result of this exercise.
- Ask yourself what qualifications the employer thinks you need. Make a list of these.
- Ask yourself what experience the employer thinks you need. Make a matching list of your own experience.
- Ask yourself what skills the employer thinks you need. Make a list of achievements that show you have these skills.
- Ask yourself what kind of person the employer is looking for. List examples to show you are that kind of person.
- Jot down the answers to any other questions you think might come up in the interview.
- Sort out well in advance what you will be wearing and what you need to take with you. Make sure the clothes you plan to wear are clean and ironed.
- Check the date and time and work out travel arrangements well in advance.
- Get to the interview in plenty of time. Use the time before the interview to run over the points you want to get across.

What should I expect when I get to the interview?

Your letter of invitation should give you some idea of the format of the interview. An interview can take one of several forms:

- An informal meeting to find out about the company.
- A one-to-one interview.
- A formal interview with a panel of interviewers.
- A group interview.
- A residential course.
- A series of tests.
- A combination of two or more of these.

Formal interviews

Most interviews follow a certain pattern:

- **Greetings and introduction:** You will probably shake hands with the interviewer(s). Listen out for the names of the people to whom you are introduced, and make sure that you sit in a comfortable position. If you have brought a briefcase or handbag into the interview, place it on the floor at your side, but make sure no one is likely to trip over it.
- **Breaking the ice:** You may be asked about the journey or the weather to give you time to settle down. Answer politely and briefly. Don't be tempted to give a lengthy account of the journey, however nightmarish it may have been.
- **Checking the facts:** You may be asked about the information on your CV. Again be polite and brief.
- **Principal question-and-answer session:** You will be asked questions to find out how suitable you are for the job.
- **Questions from the interviewee:** You will be asked if you have any questions of your own.
- **Close of interview:** You will be told what happens next and when to expect a decision. You should thank the interviewer for showing interest in your application, but do not drag this part of the interview out for too long.

How should I approach interview questions?

- Look at the person who is asking you the question, and direct your answer to him or her.

- Before you answer a question, pause for a moment to collect your thoughts. Speaking before you have worked out your answer in your head could be disastrous.
- Consider whether you have been asked a simple question about the facts, which requires a brief answer, or an open-ended question which requires you to answer the question and then elaborate.
- When answering more open-ended questions, try to elaborate your answers with one or two pieces of evidence, but avoid lengthy anecdotes.
- Stick to the point. Do not try to bring in material you have rehearsed if the question does not warrant it.
- Try to avoid speaking for more than two minutes on any individual question.
- Show that you are a good listener. In general, you should speak only for a little more than half the time.
- If you do not understand a question that is put to you, say that you do not understand, and ask for the question to be repeated.
- Do not be distracted if the interviewer takes notes while you are speaking.
- Do not be put off by long pauses after you have finished speaking. It is up to the interviewer to break the silence.

What will I get asked?

There are many angles from which interviewers can ask questions. However thorough your preparation, you are always likely to be asked something you had not envisaged. Yet there are certain questions for which you should be prepared. Think how you would answer these questions:

- What do you know about this company?
- What in particular do you feel you have to offer this company?
- What do you know about the job on offer?
- What made you apply for this particular job?

- What do you consider your strengths and weaknesses to be?
- What do you see yourself doing in five years' time?
- Why did you choose the subjects you studied at school and college?
- What did you enjoy about your college life?
- Which of your achievements has given you the greatest pleasure?
- What do you think are the most important qualities for a person taking up this position?
- What skills and experiences do you think you would be able to bring to this company?
- Do you consider yourself to be a good team member or do you prefer to work alone?
- You lack experience. How do you think you will make up for that?
- Is there any part of the job on offer that you would feel worried about doing?
- What do you think is the most effective way of motivating people?
- How do you spend your spare time?

Remember that interviewers are usually trying to find out the same information: Can you do the job? How interested are you in the job? What are your strengths and weaknesses? Would you fit into the company? What sort of a person are you?

What questions should I ask?
Before the end of the interview you should be asked if you have any questions. Have some questions for the interviewer worked out in advance. Here are some ideas:

- Ask for further information about something that is mentioned in the job advertisement.
- Pick up on something you have found out about the company in your own research. Ask how this will affect the job.
- Pick up on something that was said in the interview that you would like to be explained further.

- Ask about the company's procedures concerning assessment and promotion.
- Add any information in support of your application that you feel you have not been given the opportunity to bring out in the interview.
- Say that you did have some questions, but these were covered in the course of the interview.

Don't ask too many questions at this stage. The interviewer may well already be running late, or may be hoping to grab a cup of coffee, and could be annoyed if the interview drags on for longer than is necessary. Don't ask about holiday entitlement and pay rises. This may make you seem grasping and uninterested in doing the job for its own sake.

Group interviews

In some interviews you will be invited to take part in a discussion or activity with a group of other candidates. On such occasions you are being assessed for your ability to cooperate as much as to lead, so act accordingly:

- Don't try to dominate the discussion.
- Don't get angry or dismissive if people offer opposing views.
- Make your point clearly and then let the other candidates have their say.
- If you can't think of anything new to add, simply say that you agree with one of the previous speakers and repeat his or her point.

Residential courses

Some interviews may even involve an overnight stay, with some form of social activity included. Remember that you are being assessed for the whole of the time:

- Try to appear alert and interested at all times.
- Enjoy any social activities that are laid on, but...
- Don't get drunk in the hotel bar.

Tests

Some employers use tests to find out more about the candidates. If you are invited to take a test at the interview, make sure that you are well prepared:

- Study the invitation to the interview and find out what form the test will take.
- Revise or practise for the test as appropriate.
- Follow the usual guidelines for taking examinations (see pages 30-6).

How do I create a good impression at interview?

- Knock before entering the interview room.
- Do not sit down before you are invited to do so.
- Sit in a comfortable and upright position.
- Avoid scratching, tapping your feet, or any other irritatating habit.
- Make eye contact with the interviewer.
- Smile.
- Nod to express agreement or enthusiasm.
- Vary the tone of your voice to make it more expressive.
- Stay polite and attentive.
- Do not smoke.
- Do not accept offers of hot drinks or alcohol during the interview.
- Do not swear, even if the interviewer does.
- Do not let any informality on the part of the interviewer lull you into a false sense of security.

You can find out more about successful job seeking in *Collins Pocket Reference Finding a Job* (HarperCollins, 1996).

GUIDE TO COLLINS DICTIONARIES AND THESAURUSES
The Authority on Current English

Collins Shorter English Dictionary

The ideal dictionary for everyday use.
- Comprehensive coverage of today's language in a handy format.
- Usage notes give special help with difficult or confusable words.
- Etymologies show the history of a word's development.

98 000 references   1408 pages
ISBN 0 00 470363 4   (Hardback)

Collins College Dictionary

Up-to-date vocabulary across a wide range of subjects.
- Clear straightforward meanings.
- Examples of how words are used.
- Usage notes for extra guidance.
- Grammar supplement.

68 000 references   992 pages
ISBN 0 00 470901 2   (Vinyl)

Also available, minus grammar supplement, in paperback form as **Collins Paperback Dictionary** *ISBN 0 00 470780 X*

Collins Compact English Dictionary

The dictionary with colour for ease of use.
- Special coverage of terms used in school examination courses.
- Spelling help with all irregular and difficult forms of words.
- Word origins explained clearly and concisely.
- Language supplements.

68 000 references   1056 pages
ISBN 0 00 470267 0   (Hardback)

Collins Shorter English Thesaurus in A-Z Form
The ideal thesaurus for everyday use.
- A-Z arrangement means you can go straight to the word you want.
- Synonyms arranged in numbered lists according to meaning.
- Large clear type and easy-to-read page layout.

275 000 synonyms   768 pages
ISBN 0 00 470364 2   (Hardback)

Collins College Thesaurus

The thesaurus for students of any age.
* Alphabetical format for easy use.
* Up-to-date coverage reflects the language of today.
* Labels indicate the best context for using a word.
* Antonyms provided for many entries.

290 000 synonyms and antonyms   720 pages
ISBN 0 00 470900 4   (Vinyl)

Also available in paperback form as
Collins Paperback Thesaurus   ISBN 0 00 470779 6

Collins Compact English Thesaurus in A-Z Form

The thesaurus with colour for ease of use.
* Entry words in colour.
* Helpful labels identify areas of usage.

175 000 synonyms   768 pages
ISBN 0 00 470288 3   (Hardback)

Collins Shorter Dictionary & Thesaurus

Two books in one for everyday use.
* Dictionary entries selected for their clarity and simplicity.
* Thesaurus entries give generous synonym lists.

56 000 dictionary references & 170 000 synonyms   864 pages
ISBN 0 00 470907 1   (Hardback)

Collins Paperback Dictionary & Thesaurus

The paperback with two books in one.
* Matching dictionary and thesaurus entries on same page.
* Entry words given in colour.

40 000 dictionary references & 120 000 synonyms   720 pages
ISBN 0 00 470513 0

For full details of **Collins Dictionaries'** extensive range,
including *Pockets* and *Gems*, please contact:

Collins Dictionary Marketing Department
HarperCollins Publishers
77-85 Fulham Palace Road
Hammersmith
LONDON W6 8JB

BANK *of* ENGLISH · BANK *of* ENGLISH · BANK *of* ENGLISH · BANK *of* ENGLISH

All Collins dictionaries and thesauruses have been compiled by referring to the Bank of English, a unique database of the English language with examples of over 200 million words enabling Collins lexicographers to analyse how English is actually used today and how it is changing. This is the evidence on which the continuous updating of our texts is based.

The Bank of English was set up as a joint initiative by HarperCollins Publishers and Birmingham University to be a resource for language research and lexicography. It contains a very wide range of material from books, newspapers, radio, TV, magazines, letters, and talks reflecting the whole spectrum of English today. Its size and range make it an unequalled resource and the purpose-built software for its analysis is unique to Collins Dictionaries.

This ensures that Collins Dictionaries accurately reflect English as it is used today in a way that is most helpful to the dictionary or thesaurus user as well as including the full range of rarer and historical words and meanings.